JOURNEY OF ENDURANCE

THE PURSUIT OF GOD

VALENTINE PUBLISHING HOUSE
DENVER, COLORADO

Accident Photos - Lakewood Police Department
Cover Graphics - Desert Isle Design LLC

Publisher's Cataloging-in-Publication Data
        Journey of Endurance : The Pursuit of God — 1st ed.

        p. cm.
        Preassigned LCCN : 2001-135313
        ISBN : 0-9711536-7-1

        1. Christian life.
        2. Religious aspects — Christianity.
        3. Christian biography — United States I. Title.

        BR1725.A255A3 2002   248.2'9
                            QBI01-700781

Printed in the United States of America.

The *Journey of Endurance* is based on
actual events from the author's life.

What Others Are Saying About *The Journey*

Journey of Endurance is a life map for anyone seeking an ever-deepening walk with God.

- Warren Risch, Senior Pastor
First Covenant Church

The Journey of Endurance is profoundly down-to-earth and practical in its powerful call to personal discipleship. The author is frank and fervent in his appeal for followers of Christ to go beyond mere surface Christianity into a deep, passionate pursuit of Christ Himself.

- Dick Eastman, International President
Every Home For Christ

A profound example of Proverbs 8:17 *"...those who seek me diligently will find me."*

- Pastor Wes Sthole,
Living Tower Free Methodist

An honest story of a heart seeking God and finding Him, among other places, on skid row.

- Lon Gregg, Spiritual Director
Denver Rescue Mission

Journey of Endurance, a thought provoking adventure from a state of complacency into a never ending partnership with God.

- Stan Setliff, Senior Pastor
New Life Church

May those fortunate enough to read this work of love, embrace in their hearts the divine author of all — Jesus, Son of God.

- Father Bernard Luedtke,
Roman Catholic Priest

"Hurry!" cries the heart of God.
"Fill yourself with my powerful anointing.
I have unbelievable plans for your life.
I have chosen you to change the world."

One

⚭✝⚭

$\mathcal{A}$s I darted across all three lanes of traffic to catch the next exit, I could see the angry glare of several motorists in my rearview mirror. After a brief stop at the end of the off-ramp, I proceeded north down a steep hill. Accelerating hard in my 1980 Toyota Corolla, I passed several more vehicles as the wide-open road beckoned and my speedometer needle continued to climb.

Suddenly, a silver sports car pulled out in front of me. Apparently, the driver was trying to make a left turn and realized there wasn't enough time. He came to a complete stop, blocking my lane of traffic. By the time I hit the brakes, hundreds of feet had already passed.

As I watched my car approach his with deadly force, my perception of time came to a complete standstill. I could hear the screeching sound of tires against the pavement. A thick cloud of gray smoke streamed out from underneath my front fenders. I could see the look of terror on the other driver's face. It felt like I was watching everything in slow motion.

Within seconds of impact, I forced the steering wheel hard to the left, but it was too late. My car clipped against his with just enough force to send me into a tailspin. After a jolting blow, I watched everything flip upside down as my car spun airborne across the median.

An overwhelming panic gripped my emotions as my spirit cried out to God! A split-second later, I crashed head-on into a bright yellow school bus traveling around 45 miles per hour.

Metal tearing against metal, the impact was devastating. The front of the school bus folded in like a crushed pop can. The force ripped the engine and transmission out of my car and sent them flying toward a field a hundred yards away.

I tried to hold on, but wasn't wearing a seat belt. The impact was too great. Just as my fragile body was about to be shredded over the sharp, jagged edges of metal and glass, God appeared!

I didn't see any supernatural phenomenon, but I could feel an overwhelming sense of peace in my heart as I heard the words, "Will you endure until the end?"

Afterwards, I found myself lying on the pavement next to my front tire. Looking up, I could see a large hole where I had escaped, almost as if God ripped an opening through the side of my car and shielded my body from destruction.

I couldn't move or breathe. It felt like I had the wind knocked out of me, but with all my strength I continued to cry the Lord's Prayer aloud, over and over again.

The accident had blocked all four lanes of traffic and soon many people began to gather. They formed a circle around me and watched as I lay on the ground praying. No one approached me until the paramedics arrived. I don't know why someone didn't try to comfort me, but it was the most painful part of the accident.

After a night in the hospital, I awoke to the sound of a nurse pushing the white privacy curtain aside. She was wearing a lime-green gown and with a concerned look on her face, said, "I'm here to take you to X ray."

"Can I have something to drink?" I asked. "I'm really thirsty."

"No, the doctor said no fluids in case you have internal injuries."

As I watched the ceiling, the nurse rolled my bed down a long hall. An endless flow of white tiles and fluorescent lights passed overhead. After reaching an elevator and riding to the third floor, the nurse touched my hand and said, "Someone will be out to get you momentarily."

As I watched her walk away, I noticed a picture of Jesus made out of shiny mosaic tile on the adjacent wall. He was wearing a red robe and had one hand extended forward in blessing and the other pointed toward His heart. The white light which flowed from His heart brought tears to my eyes. Not only was I happy to be alive, but I had experienced the presence of God like never before.

I have attended church ever since I was a little boy and even say daily prayers, but this was different. It felt like I had an empty hole deep within my soul that only God could satisfy, a burning hunger that left me in search of greater meanings and accomplishments in life. I hadn't even realized the hole existed until God rescued me from the wreckage and filled my heart with

His peaceful presence.

Lying in the hospital bed with tears streaming down my face, I knew my life would be forever changed. I could never go back. Instead of going to church every Sunday and learning information about God, I wanted to experience more of His divine presence. I wanted to feel His loving, peaceful closeness once again. I had finally tasted the living water the Bible spoke about and wanted to pursue God with every fiber of my being.

Two

After I had spent several days in the hospital, my parents took me into their home and care. My mom set up a temporary bed in the living room by covering a dark green couch from the seventies with sheets and pillows. I had a great view of the television, and Mom even provided me with a radio and some Calvin and Hobbes cartoon books.

Everybody was being extremely nice to me, but after the first couple of days, my joyful enthusiasm for life and God began to fade away. Agonizing pain ripped through my body and emotions. I kept replaying the events over and over in my mind. I couldn't stop thinking about God's words, "Will you endure until the end?" The end of what? Was I to live the rest of my life a helpless paraplegic?

I was angry at the driver who stopped in my lane of traffic and at God for allowing the accident to happen in the first place. With torn ligaments in both knees, I couldn't walk. A broken collarbone prevented me from moving my left arm, and a broken thumb kept me from using my right hand.

I couldn't even get out of bed without assistance. Every day that I lay on the green couch, my condition grew worse. My knees were swollen to twice their normal size. I didn't have automobile insurance. I was probably facing a huge lawsuit from the bus driver and school district. The medical bills already exceeded twenty-five thousand dollars, and to make matters worse, I worked on commission as a loan officer and had five deals falling apart.

My breaking point came one afternoon when no one was around to help. I struggled with all my might for over an hour to get up, but it was just too painful. All I could do was lie halfway off the couch in agonizing pain.

Eventually, something inside of me snapped. I didn't care how much it hurt or if my wretched knees were torn off in the process. I grabbed the back of a chair and forced myself off the couch. Staggering through the kitchen and out the back door, I hobbled stiff-legged toward a row of lilac bushes that grew along the fence. I was so angry, I didn't even know where I was going. After making three circles around the apple tree in the center of the yard, I came back inside.

I didn't give God much credit at first, but His supernatural power healed my body that day. He even changed my attitude. My depression turned into hope, because if I could walk once, I could do it again. Within weeks the swelling in my knees decreased, and eventually I was moving around on my own. Not long after, I started taking practical steps to put my life back together.

The first order of business was my car. The impound lot was charging $20.00 a day for storage, and a man who worked there said, "Bring down your title, and we'll exchange the salvage for the towing fee." It sounded reasonable, so after locating the paperwork, I limped toward my parents' Chevy truck.

I pulled myself up into the cab, and as I left their quiet subdivision, I started realizing how fast and furiously people drive. Cars seemed to be coming toward me from all directions. I could feel terror rising up inside my throat. *What if someone cuts me off again?*

After fastening my seat belt, I was able to get my thoughts under control with the help of prayer. I tried driving extra slowly, but that only seemed to make the other drivers more aggressive. Soon they were swarming around me in an impatient rage and honking their horns.

Eventually, I arrived at the impound lot and was greeted by a man whose hands were covered in grease. "Can I help you?" he said in a gruff voice.

"I called on the phone about giving you my title."

"Which one's yours?"

"1980 Toyota Corolla."

As he flipped through a stack of paperwork behind the front counter, he paused momentarily and looked up at me with his mouth open. "That shredded pile of scrap metal's your car? There's no way anyone lived through that!"

"Yeah, I know."

"It came in here in pieces. Hey, Bill! Get in here and check out the driver of the Corolla. He's gotta be the luckiest man alive."

Soon everyone in the office was telling me how fortunate I was. I wanted to tell them about the Lord, and how He rescued me, but I was afraid. I didn't want them to laugh or think I was a religious freak, so I just smiled and agreed.

After completing the paperwork, I drove home feeling terrible. It was like I had let God down. He'd saved my life, and I was too ashamed to praise His name in public.

I barely gave God the time of day, and He rescued me from sure death. I blamed Him for the accident, and He healed my body supernaturally. Why does God love me so? I wondered. Why would the Creator of the universe be concerned with the details of my life?

During the remainder of my recovery, I started reading the Bible, as a burning hunger in my heart began to stir. I was studying the life of Paul and wondered where he got so much passion for God.

Paul started out persecuting the Christian church and ended up fighting the good fight of faith. What drove Paul to experience endless encounters with death and still keep going?

2 Corinthians 11:23-28, describes Paul's walk beautifully: *...with far greater labors, far more imprisonments, with countless floggings, and often near death. Five times I have received from the Jews the forty lashes minus one. Three times I was beaten with rods. Once I received a stoning. Three times I was shipwrecked; for a night and a day I was adrift at sea; on frequent journeys, in danger from rivers, danger from bandits, danger from my own people, danger from Gentiles, danger in the city, danger in the wilderness, danger at sea, danger from false brothers and sisters; in toil and hardship, through many a sleepless night, hungry and thirsty, often without food, cold and naked. And, besides other*

things, I am under daily pressure because of my anxiety for all the churches.

Wow, Paul was unstoppable! Without God, it would not be humanly possible for a man to suffer all that persecution and still keep going. Paul not only knew God, he lived off of God's power and strength every day. Paul's love for God conquered any obstacles that stood in his way. Fearlessly, Paul promoted the Kingdom day and night.

That's when the burning hunger in my heart began to stir into a desire for action. I wanted to experience God, just like Paul. I wanted God to use my life powerfully to make a difference in the world.

I didn't want to sit around waiting until Judgment Day before encountering God. I wanted to live the rest of my life without any more regret. I wanted a life overflowing with the peace, presence and love of Christ Himself.

Three

❧ ✝ ❧

Not knowing where to begin my journey, I decided to return to my old Bible study group. I couldn't wait to share the story of my car crash and all the exciting insights I was discovering about Paul and the first-century Christian church.

Arriving a little before 7 p.m. on Wednesday evening, I found everything as usual. Scott, Becky, Joann, Jim, Jennifer, Lisa, and Brian were sitting in a circle in Scott's basement with Bibles in hand.

"Well, look who's here," Scott said as I limped toward an empty chair.

After telling everyone how God had ripped a hole in the side of my car, I described my recent discoveries. "There's a huge difference between the first-century church and our modern-day version of Christianity," I said. "Paul was out fighting the good fight of faith. He put on the armor of God, lived for Jesus and would gladly die for Jesus.

"And not only Paul; check out Acts 5:14-16, where Peter's shadow had enough power to heal people:

Yet more than ever believers were added to the Lord, great numbers of both men and women, so that they even carried out the sick into the streets, and laid them on cots and mats, in order that

Peter's shadow might fall on some of them as he came by. A great number of people would also gather from the towns around Jerusalem, bringing the sick and those tormented by unclean spirits, and they were all cured.

"Can you imagine how much of God's powerful anointing Peter had for his shadow to heal someone? I can just imagine Peter walking down the street and zap! Instantly, the crippled man's legs became whole. After seeing the miracle, I'll bet fifty nonbelievers fell on their knees and started begging Jesus for new life."

"That happened two thousand years ago!" Brian said as he opened his Bible and read a quote from 1 Corinthians 13:8 *...as for prophecies, they will come to an end; as for tongues, they will cease; as for knowledge, it will come to an end."*

"The apostles had more power than we have today, but it doesn't exist anymore," Becky said.

"Yeah," Joann said. "I've been a believer all my life, and my shadow's never healed anyone."

"I heard the same thing on the radio the other day," Scott said. "A preacher was talking about the miracle faith healers, and he said the gifts of tongues and prophecy are no longer valid."

As everyone went around the room giving opinions, my heart broke. A scripture about how Jesus Christ is the same yesterday, today, and forever kept coming to my mind, but I didn't know where in the Bible to find it. Besides, Scott knew scripture better than anyone else, and being a seminary graduate, he also knew how to argue.

"What can I do to please God?" I said. "There has to

be something I can do with my life for all God has given me."

"You're already saved," Scott said. "Jesus came that you may have life and have it abundantly. Why not enjoy your life in its abundant fullness?"

As the group came to a close that evening, I did my best to be social and reconnect with my friends, but I couldn't stop thinking about what Joann said: "Times were different. God gave the apostles extra power because they had to build the church. Now all we have to do is confess Jesus Christ as our personal Lord and Savior."

Her words sounded attractive and alluring, but after reading about Paul and encountering God's presence, I knew there was more. I still had a burning desire to do something, but I didn't know what. I attended church every Sunday, listened to Christian music, read my Bible and even volunteered at social events. I didn't know of anything else to do, until I came across a quote from Luke 6:38.

...give, and it will be given to you. A good measure, pressed down, shaken together, running over, will be put into your lap; for the measure you give will be the measure you get back.

I had experienced the power of this quote several years earlier when I purchased a small house in northwest Denver. It was located next to a busy intersection, had red siding and a white, three-tab roof. It was my plan to turn the property into a duplex by renting the top half of the house and building an apartment in the basement.

After closing, I couldn't wait to start construction. I

built a dividing wall alongside the stairwell leading into the basement. After running an ad, I rented the top half to a family with teenage children.

Construction on the basement progressed steadily for several months, until one day when everything came to a screeching halt. It was around the first of the month when my tenants said, "We're not paying rent anymore because you're making too much noise in the basement. Go ahead and start the eviction process! It's going to take you six months to get rid of us."

I was devastated! I needed their rent to make the mortgage payment that month. I only had $287 to my name and didn't know anyone who would loan me $500.

With nowhere else to turn, I took all my money and put it in the church collection basket. The situation seemed so hopeless, why not give God a try? If nothing happened, at least I would have someone to blame besides myself.

After throwing $287 into the offering, things took a turn for the worse. I received an angry telephone call from my tenants, who said, "You sabotaged the dryer, and now we're going to sue you! All our stuff is ruined."

"What are you talking about?" I asked.

"We were only gone an hour, and the clothes dryer burned up our laundry. Firemen broke down the front door. You had better get over here right away."

As I arrived, the fire truck was pulling away and my harvest yellow clothes dryer was sitting in the front yard. Only now it was harvest yellow and black; it had burn marks all around the door.

After walking over for a closer look, I noticed the tenants inside the house, packing boxes. "What's going on now?" I asked.

"We're moving!"

The odor of smoke was unbearable. All the doors and windows were open, but it still burned my eyes. I couldn't stay inside for more than a few minutes at a time. Everything had the terrible stench of burnt plastic.

The next day, I met with a claims adjuster. After calculating the walls that needed to be washed and a new dryer, he said, "How does $2,800 sound?"

"Sounds great. When do I get the check?"

"Right away," he said.

I was overjoyed. The day after putting all my money in the church collection basket, God had successfully evicted my recalcitrant tenants and dropped $2,800 in my hands.

After the claims adjuster left, I was still praising God when there was a knock on the front door. A man stood on the porch, smiling. "Hi, my name is Don Yoho," he said. "I picked up your report over the police scanner. I'm a public insurance adjuster. Can I come in and talk about your claim?"

"You're too late. I settled a few minutes ago."

"Do you mind if I look at the figures?"

"Sure," I said, handing the man the paperwork.

"You settled too cheap," Don said. "They should have paid you to repaint the walls instead of washing them. If you want, I'll get you a better settlement."

After looking over his contract, I realized there was nothing to lose. Don was only charging a 10 percent commission on the additional funds collected, so I signed the agreement, and within a few weeks, he had collected an additional $2,000 for me.

I don't know why I didn't take tithing more seriously after having seen the power of God in my past. I always put money in the collection basket, but I never put God first by giving a full 10 percent. After reading a quote from Malachi 3:8-10, I decided to start giving back to God for all He had given me.

Will anyone rob God? Yet you are robbing me! But you say, "How are we robbing you?" In your tithes and offerings! You are cursed with a curse, for you are robbing me — the whole nation of you! Bring the full tithe into the storehouse, so that there may be food in my house, and thus put me to the test, says the Lord of hosts; see if I will not open the windows of heaven for you and pour down for you an overflowing blessing.

Four

$$\sim\!\!\!\sim\!\!\!\sim\!\!\!\dagger\!\!\!\sim\!\!\!\sim$$

Even though tithing was the right thing to do, I still had a hard time forcing myself to do it. My financial situation seemed hopeless. I had spent all my savings making payments on the accident bills. All but one of my mortgage deals had fallen apart, and I needed someone to represent my insurance claim before the school district filed a lawsuit.

I called on Don Yoho, to see whether he could help. He was happy to come over and talk, but first he wanted to get a copy of the accident report from the police department.

After acquiring the fourteen-page report, Don met me at a park by my house. "How did you explain the fact that I was uninsured?" I asked, after limping over to greet him.

"I didn't," Don said. "The driver of the silver Fiero has $300,000 in coverage, and they picked up a slight amount of alcohol on his Breathalyzer test."

"I'm worried about the bus driver."

"You should be. The poor lady had to be cut out with a rip saw. The steering wheel came down into her lap, and the metal surrounding the floorboard crushed her feet. Just consider yourself lucky there weren't any children on board."

"Are they going to sue me?"

"Don't worry, if the school district points the finger at you, we're going to pass the blame along to the driver who cut you off."

During the rest of the week, Don worked the case. He wanted me to see another doctor to get a disability report, because the ligaments in my knees were heavily damaged. There was a good chance they would never function properly again.

During this time, I prayed with more fervency than ever before. Every day I cried out for God's intervention. Then one sunny afternoon, Don called with great excitement in his voice. "I got you $60,000!"

"Wow, I can't believe it!"

"It may take a few days because of the amount. The claims adjuster needs to get a second signature on the check, but by next week you should be rolling in the dough."

God sure was being good to me! In my attempt to give back to Him financially, He turned the tables and blessed me abundantly. He opened up the heavens and good measure, pressed down, shaken together and running over, flowed into my bank account. After paying my bills off, I ended up with $30,000.

I wanted to invest the money in real estate. I knew of several loan officers who bought condemned property, renovated the houses and made thousands of dollars on resale.

In an attempt to follow their steps, I made a map of all the lowest-priced HUD and VA homes in the Denver area. After borrowing the lockbox keys from my real estate agent, I made my first stop: a beige, two-bedroom house on Quivas Street.

The graffiti spray-painted all over the brick walls caught my attention from a distance. It looked like it had been a crack house or a gang hangout before the government came along and boarded up the windows with plywood.

From the inside, it looked like the roof had been leaking for years. Large sections of the stucco ceiling had broken loose and fallen to the floor. The walls were stained by water marks, and the moisture had caused the hardwood floors to buckle in places. The kitchen had been totally destroyed. All of the cabinets had been ripped off the walls, and all that was left was a garbage disposal and some pipes protruding from the floor.

When it came time to inspect the basement, I made it halfway down the stairs before turning around and running back outside. The place gave me the creeps. Without any lights, the boarded-up house was dark, cold and damp.

After inspecting the rest of the houses on my list, I decided to buy the property on Quivas Street, because it had the best price-per-square-foot. My real estate agent submitted a bid to HUD, and to my surprise, I was awarded the property.

Immediately after closing, I went to work. I poured a concrete driveway on one side of the house and built a three-foot picket fence in the front yard. I found a great deal on large buckets of mistinted paint, and after mixing everything together, I painted the outside of the house gray with white and mauve trim. I picked up beige carpet, kitchen cabinets and appliances from an auction and reworked the interior.

Finally, the project was completed! It looked great and only took me six months. I put the house back on the market and had an offer within a week.

I sure felt blessed sitting across from the buyers at the closing table. I owned the property free and clear, and the title company gave me all the proceeds in one large check. When I got home, I carefully calculated the construction costs and deducted them from my earnings. I wanted to tithe a full 10 percent of what I made and was able to distribute $1,938 between my church and other charitable organizations.

I could feel God's mighty hand on my endeavors, bestowing His blessings on me as described in Deuteronomy 28:1-8: *If you will only obey the Lord your God, by diligently observing all his commandments that I am commanding you today, the Lord your God will set you high above all the nations of the earth; all these blessings shall come upon you and overtake you, if you obey the Lord your God: Blessed shall you be in the city, and blessed shall you be in the field. Blessed shall be the fruit of your womb, the fruit of your ground, and the fruit of your livestock, both the increase of your cattle and the issue of your flock. Blessed shall be your basket and your kneading bowl. Blessed shall you be when you come in, and blessed shall you be when you go out. The Lord will cause your enemies who rise against you to be defeated before you; they shall come out against you one way, and flee before you seven ways. The Lord will command the blessing upon you in your barns, and in all that you undertake...*

It felt good to give back to God for all He had given

me, but the financial pressures of everyday life kept pursuing me. I didn't want to spend any of my investment capital, because if I ran out of money, I would be out of business. Besides, something inside kept pushing me toward bigger and better deals.

Within a short time, I found myself buying and selling three to four properties a year. I hired two employees to help do the work and even started dating a real estate agent, who gave me a kickback on her commissions.

Life was going great, but I still wanted more. My soul was hungry for something — more money, greater excitement, bigger challenges — I didn't know what, but I started setting higher levels of achievement for myself.

Instead of setting goals for how much money I would make in a year, I set goals for how much money I would tithe in a year. I started with a goal to give $10,000 to charity, and my income level that year exceeded my expectations. Year after year, I set higher tithing goals and continued exceeding my expectations. The more I increased the amount of my tithe, the more God blessed my endeavors.

Eventually real estate prices started increasing, and I could no longer buy HUD houses cheap enough to make the profit I wanted, so I started buying vacant land. I found a partially completed townhouse project in Roxborough Park. Four units had already been built and the tap fees had been paid. The site had sat vacant for a long time and was overgrown with weeds. The bank that owned the property kept reducing the price. They were asking $65,000, so I offered them $40,000, and to my surprise, they accepted my bid.

After closing, I hired an architect to draft a new set of building plans. He created a better design, and after pulling the permits, I put together a small construction crew. We worked twelve to fourteen hours a day, framing units, installing cedar siding, clad windows, and a slate tile roof, while the electricians and plumbers worked inside.

Halfway through the project, I ran out of money. I was scared to death of losing everything. The subcontractors were expecting to be paid. Materials were being delivered, and the invoices kept piling up. I was under tremendous pressure.

Crying out with all my might, I petitioned the Lord for help. I needed a construction loan, but the banks refused to help. Everything seemed hopeless. Then one day, a silver Cadillac arrived at the job site. A tall man with a mustache stepped out of the car and said, "I'm looking for the developer."

"That would be me."

"Aren't you kind of young to be doing this?"

Looking down at the ground, I noticed a piece of wood with a nail sticking up. As I bent down to pick it up, the man extended his hand and said, "My name is Bill Elkins. I'm the private investor you called a couple weeks ago. Are you still looking for a loan?"

"More than ever. Three of the units are under contract, but they won't close until I get the certificate of occupancy from the building department."

"Why did you run out of money?"

"I didn't spend a lot of time calculating the cost, I

just bought the land and started building."

"When we spoke last, you needed $180,000. Do you think that will be enough?"

"That will get me through this phase."

"I'll need a deed of trust in first place position, 18 percent and three points," he said.

As Elkins drove away, I was overjoyed. God had come through once again. The rate was high, but Bill loaned me the money immediately. I was able to pay the subcontractors and hire more drywallers, while my crew painted the interiors and installed the kitchen cabinets. Eventually, all the units in phase one sold, and I was able to make my tithing goal of $30,000 that year.

After completing the second phase of the townhouse project, I considered myself financially retired. I tithed $50,000 to charitable organizations my last year of business and gave all the glory and credit to God.

I had everything I needed: a nice house, a new truck, a black Corvette, a boat and a beautiful girlfriend. I was set for life and never needed to work again. All I had to do was invest my money in the stock market, and at 10 percent interest, my finances would double themselves every ten years.

Five

After making a decision to get out of the construction industry, I sold all my equipment by running ads for the backhoe, loader and lumber truck. I sold the smaller tools, the air compressors, ladders and scaffold at an auction.

I wanted to consolidate all my money into one large brokerage account. I felt myself drawn to the commodities market, because I had developed a spectacular trading system.

I used the daily composite information from the NYSE and ran the numbers through a mathematical formula. It gave me a signal to go long or short for the following day. The system worked great on paper, averaging over a 400 percent return.

Because God had inspired me with the idea, I wanted to put Him first with the proceeds. I had previously tithed 10 percent to charity and paid 38 percent to the government in taxes. It didn't seem fair. I wanted to put God first, so I made a commitment to tithe 40 percent to charitable organizations.

I wanted to use the money to help the poorest of the poor. Just like Robin Hood, I wanted to use my trading system to rob the Wall Street sharks of their fortunes and give 40 percent away to starving villagers in Africa.

Within the first week of trading, I made over $10,000. The following week I experienced some minor losses, but by the third week, I was up $25,000.

The trading continued to produce phenomenal results, until one day, the market turned against me. It was a gloomy afternoon when my broker called and said, "You have a loss on paper, but it doesn't become real unless you sell."

"What if the market keeps going against me?"

"It could also turn around," he explained.

Not knowing what to do, I held my position. It was extremely stressful. I couldn't eat or sleep. I watched the computer screen from the second the market opened until the closing bell. Every day I lost more and more money.

It seemed hopeless. All I could do was pray things turned around, but they never did. I was trading in denial. Before I knew it, I had lost more than a quarter of a million dollars.

Emotionally devastated, I wanted to die. It was more than just losing all my hard-earned money. It felt like I'd lost the best part of my life which I'd used to acquire the money. The pain was unbearable. It consumed my every thought. It hurt so badly I couldn't stay in my house anymore, because I did my trading from an upstairs bedroom office.

At the advice of my pastor, I took a spiritual retreat. I left immediately and drove like a madman to the church's mountain retreat facility. I was furious with God! How dare He allow this to happen! I wanted to help the poorest of the poor, and now everything was ruined.

As I approached the retreat center, a magnificent stone church on the edge of the property caught my attention. It was built on a large rock that overlooked a calm lake. The main building was located west of the church and was surrounded by thirty-foot pine trees, aspen groves and streams of running water.

In the background, tall mountain peaks were reaching toward the heavens. Upon seeing them, I decided that's where I wanted to have it out with the Almighty.

After checking into my room, I laced up my hiking boots and headed for the highest point. I blasted through the forest like a locomotive over stumps and through trees. I climbed with my hands and feet, burning up all my anger.

After reaching the highest peak, I cried out for hours. I felt hurt, betrayed and abandoned. My life was destroyed, and God was nowhere to be found. All I could hear was the restless whisper of the cold mountain breeze.

Later that day, I found myself crying my eyes out, in pure agony, with my face to the floor. I had been self-employed my whole life, and look where it had gotten me — broken and crushed. In that moment of desperation, I came to a point of complete surrender before the Lord God Almighty.

I offered Him my life. "Take everything!" I said. "I surrender all that's left unto your service." Instantly, a peaceful feeling came over me! It felt like the time God rescued me from the deadly wreckage. I didn't hear any words of instruction, but the Lord touched my heart with a desire to write a book.

A book? I wondered as I lay on the floor wiping tears from my eyes.

"But Lord, I don't even like to *read* books." I dropped out of high school, never learned grammar and couldn't spell to save my life. Even so, I picked myself up off the floor and immediately noticed a night-and-day difference in how I felt. One minute, I was emotionally devastated, and the next, I was full of joy.

The peaceful feeling continued to fill my heart as I drove home the following day. I knew the message was from the Lord, and He even gave me a theme for the book. It was going to be about the most valuable lessons in life. Lessons that are not taught in schools.

I was a little worried about my calling, but the Lord obviously knew what He was doing; besides, I didn't have a choice. I now considered myself God-employed. When I surrendered my self-employed life over to the Lord, I became His obedient servant.

I started by making a list of the most valuable lessons in life. My teachers had taught me a lot of history and how Napoleon III was emperor of France, but no one taught me about love and happiness.

I had also learned how single-celled organisms reproduced through binary fission in my science class, but never about self-forgiveness or how to work through the steps of grieving when disaster strikes.

I also wanted my book to be spiritual, because when the most valuable lessons in life are researched deeply enough, they always reflect back to God. I wanted my book to be biblically based and soon began researching Scripture like never before.

It was then I realized the meaning of James 4:13-15: *Come now, you who say, "Today or tomorrow we will go to such and such a town and spend a year there, doing business and making money." Yet you do not even know what tomorrow will bring. What is your life? For you are a mist that appears for a little while and then vanishes. Instead you ought to say, "If the Lord wishes, we will live and do this or that."*

The verse hit me like a ton of bricks. When I was self-employed, I made all my decisions based on money. I bought property for a certain price, hired and fired employees based on the money it cost me, relative to the workload they produced. My business consumed ten to twelve hours of my time every day, and I only gave God a half-hour of prayer — *if* time permitted.

After surrendering my life to the Lord, I realized that money had been my god. The dollar had been lord over my life, because that's what influenced my decisions. Now that I had given Him every hour of every day for the rest of my life, I saw the difference between confessing the Lord with my mouth and actually making Him Lord of my life.

I was so excited about this discovery, I wanted to share the information with all of my friends. When Wednesday night rolled around, I headed over to Scott's house. I hadn't been to Bible study for about three months, but everyone seemed glad to see me.

Scott lived in a light blue house in a subdivision close to mine. When I arrived, he greeted me with a big hug and said, "Welcome, brother, I've been praying for you. How are things going?"

"You won't believe what happened to me. Do you know the quote from Romans where Paul is talking about living and dying for the Lord? Well, I made a huge discovery. Do you mind if I share it with the group tonight?"

"That would be great; we just finished our study on Philemon."

After everyone had gathered in a circle in Scott's basement, Scott opened with prayer and directed the conversation towards me. I felt uncomfortable at first, but was able to describe to them how I had lost everything trading commodities. I could barely speak the words without reliving the pain all over again.

"But there's also good news," I said. "For the first time in my life I actually surrendered my life to Jesus. Sure, I said the words with my mouth, *Lord Jesus, I confess you as my Lord and Savior.* But I never totally committed my life to His service.

"It was a night-and-day difference. Before, I would pray for help solving my problems. I wanted God to line His will up with my agenda. Now I'm aligning my will up with God's agenda.

"And there's more. Check out the parable from Luke 19:12-27:

...a nobleman went to a distant country to get royal power for himself and then return. He summoned ten of his slaves, and gave them ten pounds, and said to them, "Do business with these until I come back." But the citizens of his country hated him and sent a delegation after him, saying, "We do not want this man to rule over us." When he returned, having received royal power, he ordered

these slaves, to whom he had given the money, to be summoned so that he might find out what they had gained by trading. The first came forward and said, "Lord, your pound has made ten more pounds." He said to him, "Well done, good slave! Because you have been trustworthy in a very small thing, take charge of ten cities."

Then the second came, saying, "Lord, your pound has made five pounds." He said to him, "And you, rule over five cities." Then the other came, saying, "Lord, here is your pound. I wrapped it up in a piece of cloth, for I was afraid of you, because you are a harsh man; you take what you did not deposit, and reap what you did not sow." He said to him, "I will judge you by your own words, you wicked slave! You knew, did you, that I was a harsh man, taking what I did not deposit and reaping what I did not sow? Why then did you not put my money into the bank? Then when I returned, I could have collected it with interest."

He said to the bystanders, "Take the pound from him and give it to the one who has ten pounds." (And they said to him, "Lord, he has ten pounds!") "I tell you, to all those who have, more will be given; but from those who have nothing, even what they have will be taken away. But as for these enemies of mine who did not want me to be king over them — bring them here and slaughter them in my presence."

"This parable applies to me because I'm the slave who didn't want anyone ruling over his life. I used the majority of my life for financial gain. I never used it to serve the Lord's agenda, only my own.

"And did you hear what happens to those who don't want Jesus ruling over their lives? They are slaughtered in His presence! I can't believe you guys didn't tell me about this!"

"Jesus is not going to slaughter anyone," Joann said

31

in a defensive tone. "Jesus loves you!"

"I think you're missing my point. I had been serving the god of money all these years and after losing everything, my eyes are finally open. Don't you see what I'm talking about?"

"I don't think God cares how we earn a living so long as we believe in Jesus," Scott said. "Just look at John 3:16. *For God so loved the world that he gave his only Son, so that everyone who believes in him may not perish but may have eternal life.*"

"The lesson cost me a quarter of a million dollars, and it changed my life. I only want you guys to benefit from it as well."

"Benefit from what?" Joann asked.

"Let me do more research and maybe I can explain it better next week."

"Sounds good to me," Scott said.

Six

The following day, I stopped by the library to work on my book project. The city had just completed a state-of-the-art facility in lower downtown Denver. It had seven levels, private study rooms and a more extensive reference section than any other library in the state.

I needed more information on the forgiveness process, so I went to the computer to start my research. I found a book called *Forgiving Your Spouse After an Affair* and *Forgiveness — The Key to a Happy Life*, but nothing that had universal steps to follow. After several hours, I checked out the books I thought looked best, intending to condense the information they contained into clearly defined steps.

After a lot of research, I developed a two-part healing process. The first step required the individual to write a letter to himself, embracing his painful emotions and completely purging all negativity from his soul.

The second part of the process required the individual to find a way to love the hurt part of himself. Love is what heals people, and because God is the source of love, the process would involve prayer and complete surrender to God's love.

I wanted to test the healing process myself and decided to embrace my pain from the stock market loss. Every time a market report came over the evening news, I relived the same sick feelings over and over again. I had been stuffing the emotions back down, trying to distract myself with anything that would make me feel better, but now it was time to face my pain head-on.

After a lot of prayer, I took pencil and paper in hand and began writing a letter to my past self. It seemed like my present self, (the guy who lost all his money) was angry at my past self for making the fatal commodities trades.

I envisioned how my past self was sitting behind the computer buying and selling highly leveraged positions. I started calling him names. I wrote down all the reasons why I was angry. I vented all my negative emotions and told my past self how stupid he had been for gambling and not testing the system more thoroughly.

After I vented all the negative emotions that were trapped deep within my soul, I imagined how my past self looked lying on the mountain retreat facility's floor. He was broken and crushed. He didn't need anyone screaming angry words at him, he felt bad enough. He needed someone to get down and embrace his pain. He needed love.

As the feelings in my heart began to shift, I started writing down all the loving words my past self needed to hear. I told him about all his good qualities and all the positive things he had going. After writing several paragraphs my heart shifted completely, and my present self was able to feel compassion for my past self.

For the first time since the loss, I was able to love my complete self.

I realized there was no longer any reason to beat myself up. I hadn't lost the money on purpose. It was a mistake. I was doing the best I could.

Suddenly, I started crying and was able to feel God's love filling the emptiness in my heart. It was the same love I had encountered the day of the car crash.

As I lay on the floor crying, I began apologizing for my mistakes and asking God to help me pick up the pieces. I apologized for the way I had disrespected His holy name on the way to the retreat facility. I apologized for not making Him Lord over my finances and for losing all the money He had given me.

It was such a powerful experience, I continued researching the subject of forgiveness. As I did, I noticed many negative feelings about my father that were interfering with my peace of mind.

I love my parents dearly, but when I was growing up, my father was very critical of everything. It felt like he never had anything good to say about me. Nothing I did ever seemed good enough. I hardly ever received any positive affirmations or a sense of self-worth from him.

As a little boy, I desperately wanted my father's love and approval. I always looked up to him with admiration and aspired to be just like him. I depended on him for my existence and survival. So when he lashed out at me with critical words, I was deeply hurt. His negative remarks cut deep into my soul and remained there ever since.

I needed to heal the hurt within my heart, even though I had forgiven my father with words from my mouth a long time ago. We always got along on family outings, we talked and spent time together. I loved my father, but deep in my heart the hurt was still there.

I was tired of repressing my true feelings, so once again, I turned to the healing process. I began with a lot of prayer. I asked God to soften my heart and to allow His healing love to enter. As God began working, I wrote the following letter:

Dear Dad,

I'm writing you this letter to express and vent my angry feelings. You were very negative and critical all during my childhood. You never had anything nice to say to me, and it hurts! Why didn't you ever tell me how much you cared? All I wanted was your love and approval. I looked up to you. You were my everything. I'm angry. I didn't deserve to be treated like that! I'm sad because I wanted a loving father. I'm sad because I wanted your love and approval, and I never received it.

I wish we could go back and change the past. I'm sorry I didn't meet your expectations. I'm sorry we didn't have a closer relationship. I'm sorry for any wrong I have caused you. I know you didn't mean to hurt me. I know you were a sweet innocent little boy (just like me) who was hurt by your own critical father. I'm sorry that you suffered the same way I did. Let's rebuild our relationship. I love you.

Signed, your son

After I wrote this first letter, I wanted to hear my dad apologize and validate my feelings. It didn't matter if my dad felt like apologizing or not, I hadn't deserved to be treated like that. I knew if my father was in a completely healed state, full of God's love, he would apologize in a second, so I decided to write an imaginary response letter on his behalf.

Instead of writing words he might actually say, I needed to write the words that I deserved to hear. It was my hurt, and I was responsible to bring healing into my own life, so I wrote the following letter to myself, on his behalf:

Dear Son,

I'm so sorry. I never knew how badly I hurt you. I did the best I could. I wanted to be the best father in the world for you. I'm sorry, I tried my best. I never meant to hurt you with my negative comments. All I wanted was for you to grow up and be the best you could be. Please don't hold this against me. I'm sorry, please forgive me. I understand how you feel. I grew up with a very critical father myself. I love you a lot. I'm very proud of you. You mean the world to me.

Signed, your Dad

After I wrote this letter on my father's behalf, my hardened heart started melting. At first I couldn't believe I wrote it. As I continued to read it over and over, I broke down and started crying. The words moved from my head to my heart, and I was able to accept my father's love and forgive him.

An enormous hurt that I carried around for years was gone, and God's love now resided in its place. It was such a powerful experience I felt physically lighter afterwards. I couldn't wait to tell everyone at Bible study.

Seven

Several hours before the Wednesday night group, I found myself unprepared. I had been working hard on the healing exercise all week and didn't have any time to do the research I had promised Scott. I wanted to show him why it's important to make Jesus Lord over his life, but I only had time to look up a few quotes.

As I pulled up in front of Scott's house, Becky was getting out of her car. She waited for me to park, and after coming over to greet me, she said, "Your story about the stock market loss broke my heart. I'm sorry it happened; but why are you writing a book? It's almost impossible to get published these days."

"When I surrendered my life to Jesus, I became His obedient servant."

"I used to work for a large New York house. They received hundreds of manuscripts every day, all of which were unsolicited and rejected. Many were well written, and I'm sure the authors worked on them for years. If you're not a pastor of a megachurch or don't have an established audience or radio show, there's just no money in publishing."

"I'm sure the Lord has a plan. Besides, I don't have a choice. All I can do is walk in obedience."

Once we were inside, Scott began the Bible study by saying, "Let's all turn to the twenty-first chapter of Numbers. There you'll find the Israelites breaking faith with God. They were sick of eating manna in the wilderness and started complaining. God sent poisonous serpents, and many of the Israelites died. After Moses interceded for the people, God had him make a bronze serpent and mount it on a pole. Anyone who looked at it with faith was healed.

"Now let's turn to John 3:14-16, where it says: *And just as Moses lifted up the serpent in the wilderness, so must the Son of Man be lifted up, that whoever believes in him may have eternal life. For God so loved the world that he gave his only Son, so that everyone who believes in him may not perish but may have eternal life.*

"The scripture's clear," Scott said. "Just as the Israelites looked at the bronze serpent and believed, so all we need to do is look at Jesus and believe."

"That's what you said last week," I said. "I told you how I made Jesus Lord of my life, and you told me all I needed was a belief; but what good is a mere belief? Everyone believes something about Jesus. Some people believe Jesus was a great prophet. The Jewish leaders believed He was a troublemaker, so they killed Him.

"Even the demons believe in Jesus. In James 2:19, it says, *...the demons believe - and shudder.* And in Mark 5:7, a demon calls Jesus *Son of the Most High God.* Surely the demons know Jesus died on the cross for sins, but they're not going to Heaven."

"Look up Romans 10:13 for yourself," Scott said. *For, 'Everyone who calls on the name of the Lord shall be saved!'*

That's what the Bible says, and I'm standing on the word of God! We're saved by faith in Jesus! I'm sorry you lost all your money in the stock market, but it has nothing to do with the theological concepts of Christianity."

"I don't see it like that."

"Maybe you need to study the Bible more often."

"Maybe we're talking about the same thing," I said, trying to avoid an argument. "Let's look at how we're defining the word *belief*. In John 14:12, Jesus defines *belief* as follows: *Very truly, I tell you, the one who believes in me will also do the works that I do and, in fact, will do greater works than these...* That's because if you truly believe Jesus is the Son of God, you will obey all His commandments and make Him Lord over your life."

"Now you're talking about works," Scott said. "All have fallen short of keeping His commands, and that's why we need a savior."

"If the only requirement for the Christian walk is a belief, why did the Lord call me to write a book after I surrendered my life to Him? Maybe I'm way off course, or maybe you're twisting the quote from Romans out of context? Either way, I'm going to do some research and get back to you."

"Do all the research you want," Scott said, changing the subject to prayer requests.

After leaving Scott's house that evening, I kept reading the quote from Romans 10:12-14. *For there is no distinction between Jew and Greek; the same Lord is Lord of all and is generous to all who call on him. For, "Everyone who calls on the name of the Lord shall be saved."*

Eventually, I noticed the quotation marks setting off the verse in question and realized Paul was quoting the statement directly from Joel 2:32. He was using an Old Testament quote to make a point to an audience in Rome.

Knowing that God's word never changes in meaning and that Paul, being a Jewish Pharisee, would never twist scripture out of context to make a point, I went back to read Joel 2:32, to gain an understanding of the original meaning.

The prophet Joel was describing a future event when God would pour out His spirit on all flesh. I'm sure the Jews, God's chosen race, took this message offensively because Gentiles were considered unholy and totally cut off from God.

Once I understood the proper context of Joel 2:32, I was able to carry the same meaning forward, and it finally made sense. Paul was addressing a Jewish and Gentile audience in Rome, saying, don't be surprised that everyone is included in God's plan for salvation, because even the prophet Joel spoke about a time when God would pour out His spirit on all flesh. Paul never intended to say a *call* was the only requirement to enter the salvation process, or that whoever *calls* is guaranteed eternal life.

Scott had twisted the scripture out of context and failed to see the need for making Jesus Lord of his life. It grieved my heart, so I called him on the phone and said, "Hey Scott, do you have a minute?"

"Sure, what's up?"

"After researching Romans, I have discovered the

difference between quotes that talk about the salvation message and those that describe the salvation process."

"I'm listening," he said.

"I started thinking how the Jews were God's chosen race. God delivered them from slavery, established His covenant with them, gave them the Ten Commandments and the Law of Perfection Rituals. He traveled with them in a cloud by day and a pillar of fire by night. They were His holy people, whom He loved and protected.

"Then one day the carpenter's son starts healing people. He called the highly respected religious leaders *whitewashed tombs*, He spoke in confusing parables, and told His followers how they have to eat His flesh and drink His blood. He called himself God's Son, and finally the Jews killed Him for blasphemy.

"After His death and resurrection, the apostles had to go after the lost sheep and sell them on the Messiah. They had to tell the Jews to put aside their God-given purification rituals and follow a new way called Jesus. Not an easy job."

"Probably why all the apostles were martyred," Scott said. "But what's your point?"

"Some passages talk about the salvation message and others talk about the salvation process. There's a big difference.

"The quote, *'Everyone who calls on the name of the Lord shall be saved,'* comes from Joel 2:32. The emphasis is on the word *everyone*. Paul is explaining why the salvation process is open to both Jews and Gentiles alike. It has more to do with the message of salvation than the salvation process.

"And that quote from John 3:16, *For God so loved the world that he gave his only Son, so that everyone who believes in him may not perish but may have eternal life,* it's describing the purpose of Jesus' mission. The gospel writer's not listing the necessary requirements for the salvation process. Do you see the difference?"

"Not really. What are you trying to say?"

"My point's simple. Jesus needs to be Lord over every aspect of your life. Just like Luke 6:46-49 says: *Why do you call me "Lord, Lord," and do not do what I tell you? I will show you what someone is like who comes to me, hears my words, and acts on them. That one is like a man building a house, who dug deeply and laid the foundation upon a rock; when a flood arose, the river burst against that house but could not shake it, because it had been well built. But the one who hears and does not act is like a man who built a house on the ground without a foundation. When the river burst against it, immediately it fell, and great was the ruin of that house.*"

"That parable can be interpreted many different ways," Scott said.

"All I'm asking you to do is lift it up in prayer. Allow Jesus to show you the truth."

"I didn't want to waste the group's time on this, but if you insist, I'll research the Greek for next week's meeting. Maybe then you'll understand what I'm talking about," Scott said.

"Whatever it takes. See you later."

Eight

In the days to come I continued working on the forgiveness process and decided to tell my father about the letters I had written. He sounded interested, so I explained the two-part process of venting negative emotions and replacing them with love. After I described the emotional freedom I was experiencing, he invited me over the following evening.

Arriving a little early, I sat in my car for a long time, looking at their red brick ranch from behind two maple trees that grew in their front yard. I found myself scared to go inside because I had asked my father to write a list of the most traumatic experiences he had encountered during his childhood.

After summoning my courage, I walked through the front door and said, "Hi Dad, how's it going?"

"I only came up with a few things. But after thinking about it, this letter writing is not going to work. It happened a long time ago. Why dig up dirt from the past after it's been buried for years?"

"Because if you don't scare the skeletons out of your closet, they remain trapped inside forever."

"But I don't like writing letters. Life on the farm wasn't easy for anyone."

"You don't have to write them if you don't want to. Writing only helps bring up memories and makes the healing process more manageable. You can also heal by using visualization techniques. Just close your eyes and tell me what happened. Try to picture the events in your mind and reexperience the feelings as you describe the details."

"It happened back in North Dakota, when I was eight years old. I was helping my father dry potatoes in the sun. We had to store them in the cellar all winter, and if they weren't completely dry, they would start growing sprouts.

"The potatoes were sitting on a wooden flatbed trailer when it started to rain. We needed to push the trailer back into the barn, so I offered to steer. I didn't take a big enough turn, and the front wheel hit the side of the barn door. My father got mad, grabbed a two-by-four and started beating me with it."

"Stay with the scene and tell me where the little boy is now," I prompted.

"He's lying on the ground crying, trying to cover his head with his hands."

"Let's pretend we have a time machine and go back to the farm in North Dakota. Can you pick that little boy off the ground and imagine what he looks like?"

"Yes," he whispered.

"Why don't you hold him in your arms and tell him it's not his fault. Tell him no one deserves to be hit like that. Tell him how proud you are of him for helping with the trailer. I'm sure he did the best he could."

As I spoke these words to my father, tears began rolling down his cheeks. "What's going on now?" I asked.

"The little boy feels better, but my father's still standing there with the board in his hands."

"Why don't you take the little boy over to your father and tell him how you feel. Tell him it's wrong to hit a child. Take the two-by-four out of his hands and break it in half. It's important to vent all your angry emotions. Allow the hurt child to express his fears and feelings of inadequacy."

"Yeah, that feels much better," my father said, as he continued working through his negative emotions.

"Now why don't you have your father get down on his knees and apologize. Have your father speak all the words you deserve to hear."

A steady stream of tears began rolling down my father's face. Hearing him talk about my grandfather made me cry as well. It was a bonding moment. God showed up and healed us both, as we sat in the living room feeling love for one another and for all the hurt we had unjustly suffered in the past.

After several hours of healing work, my father was emotionally drained. We were able to get through one more incident and started talking about all the emotional abuse that accompanied my grandfather's physical abuse.

It was then I realized the meaning of Exodus 34:6-7: *...The Lord, the Lord, a God merciful and gracious, slow to anger, and abounding in steadfast love and faithfulness, keeping steadfast love for the thousandth generation, forgiving iniquity and transgres-*

sion and sin, yet by no means clearing the guilty, but visiting the iniquity of the parents upon the children and the children's children, to the third and the fourth generation.

My grandfather's emotional and physical abuse had been passed on to my father's generation. If my grandfather had repented of his sinful actions, I'm sure God in His great mercy would have forgiven him, but by no means did God remove the destructive consequences. It was all passed down the generational bloodline.

My father never hit me, but the abuse continued in the form of negative put-downs, sarcasm and criticism. I inherited the same sins, and became the third generation.

I was very critical when I was growing up, and if I didn't break the cycle by writing my forgiveness letters, I would pass the same sin on to my own children.

After leaving my father's house that evening, I started praising God for helping us heal. My eyes had been opened to the healing process, and I couldn't wait to share the information with the world. I was feeling better about the book God called me to write, and I even envisioned myself doing healing seminars. I wanted to travel around the world and bring God's healing love to all those who were wounded.

I figured the best place to start would be with my Bible study group, because there, everyone knew one another's issues. Jennifer's father was an alcoholic. Scott's parents divorced when he was five years old. I'm sure Joann would claim to have had a perfect childhood, but kids get hurt all the time. Bullies on the playground, bad dates, embarrassing or shameful moments. Life is full of hurtful events, and everyone could benefit from some healing work.

When Wednesday night rolled around, Scott was in a terrible mood. Apparently Jake, a new guy at his work, was promoted into a position that Scott wanted. He was very upset and complained about it for at least ten minutes.

"This is the perfect situation to surrender to God," I said. "You need to forgive Jake and fill yourself with God's love. Why stay stuck in bitterness?"

"It's not fair. I deserved that promotion! I've worked there for nine years, and I'm the best person for the job. It just sucks, and I don't feel like forgiving anyone."

"But lack of forgiveness only hurts the self."

"I don't care. Jake's a two-faced jerk."

"I'm sorry it happened. I have a great exercise that will help. Do you mind if I share it with the group tonight?"

"Go ahead," Scott said.

"Do you know the quote from Matthew 18:3, where Jesus says, *...Truly I tell you, unless you change and become like children, you will never enter the kingdom of heaven.*?

"As infants we are born with pure and clean emotions. God has given us our natural programming, and we all act pretty much the same. We assertively ask for our needs when we're hungry, use 90 percent of our creative abilities, learn new things at an amazing rate of speed and have very few natural fears.

"Then sooner or later bad things happen and we get hurt. If our parents are not around to give us the love and support we need, we hurt for a short time before that hurt gets repressed into our subconscious. Once the lack of forgiveness gets repressed into our subconscious, it has the power to change our God-given natural programming.

"Let me give you an example. Young children are not born with the inherent fear of bees. But if you're an adult who's afraid of bees, guess what happened in your past?"

"You got stung," Jennifer said.

"Exactly, and the same thing applies to all our God-given natural programming. Have you ever seen an abusive, alcoholic or compulsively driven baby?"

"No, we're born in the image and likeness of God," Brian said.

"Right, I was born emotionally pure and clean until my father's negativity lashed out at me and cut deep into my soul. Every time it happened I repressed the hurt I was feeling and it changed my subconscious natural programming until I became critical. That's how the sins of the father are passed down to the third and fourth generation.

"I grew up critical just like my father and wasn't able to break the generational curse until I went back and did my forgiveness work. It wasn't enough to think less-critical thoughts. I actually had to dig up all the pain of my past and invite God's love into my hurt. That's why Jesus holds our forgiveness contingent upon the way we forgive others."

"That's not true," Scott said. "Jesus came to forgive sins!"

"Then how do you explain the Lord's Prayer in

Matthew 6:12-15? *And forgive us our debts as we also have for-given our debtors... For if you forgive others their trespasses, your heavenly Father will also forgive you; but if you do not forgive oth-ers, neither will your Father forgive your trespasses.*

"Do you remember when we were talking about the difference between the salvation message and the salva-tion process?" I said. "Jesus did come to forgive sins. That's the good news. It's part of our salvation mes-sage, but it doesn't mean everyone is instantly forgiven. Turning away from sin and forgiving others is part of the salvation process. In Matthew 18:23-35, Jesus makes this point clear.

...the kingdom of heaven may be compared to a king who wished to settle accounts with his slaves. When he began the reck-oning, one who owed him ten thousand talents was brought to him; and, as he could not pay, his lord ordered him to be sold, together with his wife and children and all his possessions, and payment to be made. So the slave fell on his knees before him, saying, "Have patience with me, and I will pay you everything." And out of pity for him, the lord of that slave released him and forgave him the debt.

But that same slave, as he went out, came upon one of his fel-low slaves who owed him a hundred denarii, and seizing him by the throat, he said, "Pay what you owe." Then his fellow slave fell down and pleaded with him, "Have patience with me, and I will pay you." But he refused; then he went and threw him into prison until he would pay the debt.

When his fellow slaves saw what had happened, they were greatly distressed, and they went and reported to their lord all that had taken place. Then his lord summoned him and said to him, "You wicked slave! I forgave you all that debt because you pleaded with me. Should you not have had mercy on your fellow slave, as I had mercy on you?" And in anger his lord handed him over to be tortured until he would pay his entire debt. So my heavenly Father will also do to every one of you, if you do not forgive your brother or sister from your heart.

"Notice Jesus says *heart,* not *head.* If we don't forgive our brother or sister from the heart, we will be handed over to be tortured until we pay the entire debt. It's easy to forgive someone with pleasant words from the mouth while still holding bitterness and resentment deep in the heart. That's why this healing exercise the Lord showed me is so powerful. It will help you forgive the guy from your work, Scott."

"I don't even want to think about forgiveness right now. I'll pray about it later, and in a couple of weeks I'm sure it won't bother me anymore."

"You can stuff it down and get along with Jake, but what happens when another opportunity for promotion comes up? All those repressed feelings will come back and rear their ugly head.

"It's like if someone stole my car. I could get a new car, but if I don't forgive the thief from my heart, I'm always going to be looking over my shoulder to see if my new car's safe."

"Thanks, but no thanks. I'll be fine without your forgiveness exercise," Scott said.

"But you haven't even heard how it works."

"That's OK, we need to get back to Bible study."

Nine

~~~~~~~~✝~~~~~~~~

For many more months I worked on the book project anywhere between ten and twelve hours a day. It was scheduled to be released soon, and I believed it was going to be a best-seller because I could feel God working with me every day.

During this time, I also continued working on the forgiveness process. I had to work through everything I was writing about and found myself doing many more healing letters. I went after my own healing process with the same passion I had used making money and building townhouses.

I wrote more than a hundred letters, and issues still kept surfacing. Every time a negative memory popped up in my conscience, I felt like stuffing it back down. But instead, I took the time to work through the pain so that I could experience more of God's love.

These letters also helped me in relationships. I found myself unable to make an emotional commitment to my girlfriend because I had been hurt in the past. My heart had been ripped out and stomped upon many times, and I learned not to trust anyone or open myself up anymore. I guarded my heart with heavy walls and wouldn't let anyone inside.

Realizing this wasn't healthy and that God wanted my heart to flow freely with His love, I went back in my past and wrote healing letters to all my old girlfriends who had hurt me. Soon I became more trusting and could give and receive love more freely.

I also had to do a lot of healing in the area of public speaking. I started giving talks to different groups on the topic of forgiveness and found that I was terrified. I wasn't born with a fear of public speaking, and after a lot of prayer, I was able to trace its source back to a classroom in fourth grade, when I had to give a report in front of the entire class. Everyone started laughing at me for a mistake I made. I was devastated, and from that moment forward, I hated getting up in front of groups.

After identifying the root cause of my fear, I wrote a healing letter to my teacher, where the entire class apologized. I learned to love and comfort that frightened little boy inside and soon found myself more confident making public appearances.

I needed the added courage because the leaders of a Christian singles conference wanted me to give three workshops on the importance of healing in relationships. It was my first major speaking engagement, and I found myself extremely nervous.

On the day of the conference, I frantically drove to a shipping yard on the other side of town. My books were scheduled to arrive, and I wanted to have some available to sell afterwards. But when I entered the yard office the trucking supervisor said, "The driver had some mechanical problems late last night. Don't worry, he'll be here any minute."

Pacing back and forth on the concrete docks in front of a long row of overhead doors, I felt like I was going crazy. I wanted to get to the conference early and set up. Now, everything was ruined.

After waiting for more than an hour, I ran into the yard office and said, "When the truck gets here, will you please send a few cases of books to this location?" I quickly wrote down the address of the classroom and turned to leave.

"Sure," the man said, after I was out the door.

I only had thirty minutes to fight my way through traffic. By the time I arrived, the classroom was already filled with people. Assuming I was in the right spot, I walked in and started teaching. It's not easy sharing painful events from the past with a group of strangers, but I was able to tell everyone how I grew up with a critical father and how, because of that, I used to criticize all my girlfriends.

"My sister had suffered the same abuse, and she took it personally," I said. "When my father pointed out all her inadequacies, it made her feel worthless, and she ended up marrying a man who treated her the same way. My sister could have fifty nice guys wanting to date her, but she always went after the abusive jerk, because that's how she'd been conditioned.

"In a way, I became like my father and started abusing my relationship partners. My sister took the abuse personally and continued to draw abusive men into her life. The only way to break unhealthy childhood conditioning is to go back and do the necessary healing work."

From the back of the room a man raised his hand and said, "Is this Christian?"

"Yes, Christians are required to forgive people who hurt them."

A woman in the front row said, "You look kind of young to be doing this. What are your qualifications?"

"I have no qualifications other than God who called me to write a book and heal my repressed emotional baggage."

From there, the seminar went from bad to worse. Many people walked out before the healing exercise began. Others sat through the sound recording that gave instructions for the two-part healing letter, but I could tell by the way they were looking around the room, they were not interested. There were a few who actually embraced their pain and started crying during the exercise. I met with them afterwards and listened to their stories.

One woman had just broken up with her boyfriend and another was healing from a recent divorce. It was touching to see the joy in their eyes as they described the newfound freedom God had given them. I wanted to get feedback from everyone, but just as class let out, my books arrived.

I ripped open the box and raised the first copy to the Lord in thanksgiving. I knew what it looked like from the preliminary cover design, but holding the actual book for the first time brought an overwhelming sense of joy.

I thought everyone would want to buy one. The book was packed with phenomenal information, but very few people were willing to pay $14 for the master-piece I'd worked on for more than two years. I was only able to sell half a box during the three-day conference.

My resolve started slipping. Why did the Lord call me to write a stupid book in the first place? I could have made more money flipping burgers. I would rather eat a handful of nails than get up in front of a group and give a speech.

I tried to stay positive and look at all the good things that were happening, like the people who had been healed and the new friendships that I'd formed, but as the conference drew to a close, I found myself depressed and discouraged. Once again, I was angry at God.

As I sat on a bench outside the building, a woman with blonde hair and blue eyes came up to me and we started talking. She told me her name was Cindy. After I told her what had happened, she said, "Don't take it personal. The majority of people here are looking for someone to date. Very few are interested in self-work. I thought your seminar was great."

"Thanks, I needed to hear that. What brings you here?"

"I taught a class on spiritual warfare."

"Oh, really? What's that like?"

"I came from an abusive childhood myself. My father left when I was two years old, because my mother was a heavy alcoholic. She used to get drunk with her boyfriends and beat me. I took most of the abuse upon myself, trying to protect my little sister. After getting involved with the occult, drugs and alcohol, I ran away. I ended up in the hospital and after frequenting rehab centers for several years, I gave my life to the Lord. He delivered me from my addictions and has been working on me ever since."

"Wow, that's a powerful testimony."

"I had to go through years of deliverance and self-work to get into right relationship with the Lord. In a way, I'm glad it happened. If I hadn't come from such a terrible background, I wouldn't know the Lord as deep as I do today."

I felt an instant connection with Cindy and asked for her phone number. She was a devout Christian, and I could tell we were going to be best friends.

She took a tiny notepad from her purse and wrote down her number, then started naming Christian organizations that could help promote my book.

"Call Michele at JC-105. She'll put you on the air."

"Are you sure?"

"Let me know how it goes," Cindy said, and she gave me a hug good-bye.

Ten

The next day, I called Michele who worked as a D.J. on the local Christian radio station. After describing how I'd met Cindy at the Christian conference, she invited me down for an interview.

On the day of my appointment, I was extremely nervous and managed to arrive ten minutes early. It was a secured building, and I was greeted by a voice over the intercom that said, "Someone will be down to get you momentarily." Eventually a tall lady with long red hair came to the door and said, "Hi, I'm Michele, come on in."

I followed her to a door marked Studio B, where she took a seat behind a large black control panel. She was surrounded by monitors and stereo equipment stacked one piece on top of the other in tall towers. The walls were covered with soundproof foam, and there were shelves containing thousands of CDs, all marked with color-coded tags. As I continued to look around the room, Michele pointed towards a chair in the corner and said, "Have a seat."

"How's this going to work?" I asked.

"Put the earphones on to hear how we sound and move the microphone in front of you. We're mostly a music station, so in between songs we'll talk about your book. Get ready to do a short segment right after this break."

As the music in my headphones softly faded away I could hear Michele say, "Steven Curtis Chapman for you on this bright and sunny afternoon, and we have a very special guest in studio who's going to talk about his latest book. Stay tuned, we'll be back in a flash."

As the commercials played in the background, I could feel a burning heat sweeping over me. My hands were getting clammy and I tried to focus on my breathing, while Michele flipped through my book.

"Get ready, three, two, one...What an incredible book! I just love the cover and the table of contents. It looks like you've got a lot of great information here. Tell us about it, what inspired you? What's it all about?"

"Ah, a, it's a book on a relationships."

"What kind of relationships? And how does this healing-tool theme fit into relationships? I see some chapters here on grieving loss, love, communication and conflict resolution. What's your favorite relationship tool? And how have you used these tools in your own life?"

"Ah, a, there's a lot of a healing tools on, a, relationships."

"Stay tuned, we'll be back for the second half of the interview right after Amy Grant at JC-105."

Michele removed her headphones and looked across the control panel at me with her big brown eyes.

"You're going to have to give more than one-word answers. My boss doesn't like it when there's long, silent pauses on the radio. It's called dead air. We need to keep the conversation flowing, lively and exciting."

"I'm sorry, this is my first time."

"It's OK, you're doing fine. Tell me, what makes your book Christian?"

"It's a collection of tools to help people repair and improve relationships. Making relationships work is all about healing your own issues so they don't conflict with your partner. Prayer is an important part in that process, and that's why I talk about God in every chapter. I also have a New Covenant chapter, which helps the reader get into right relationship with God by going through His Son, Jesus Christ."

"Excellent, that's what you need to say when we go live."

The second half of the interview flowed much better. Michele was extremely confident on the air, and she took over the parts where I failed. She did an excellent job talking about my book without ever having read it, and I struggled with every word, because negative thoughts and arrows kept flying everywhere.

I could hear the condemning voices as clear as day: *You're no good. You have no qualifications. You don't know what you're talking about.* As soon as I took one negative thought captive, another would surface.

After saying goodbye to Michele that afternoon, I started dreading the future, because the P.R. firm that was working with my publisher had booked the entire week surrounding Valentine's Day with nationwide radio interviews.

On the surface, the telephone interviews sounded simple enough. All I had to do was talk on the phone about my book and the conversation would go out over the air. But when it came time to do it, the negative arrows started flying once again.

Most of the stations had mainstream audiences and were looking for romantic ideas for Valentine's Day. They wanted hot, passionate sex tips for their love-crazed listeners, and I wanted to talk about the healing process. To make matters worse, most secular stations only wanted to entertain their audience and became very defensive when I mentioned anything of a spiritual nature.

I learned this the hard way one morning on a popular oldies show. There were three hosts, Trixy, Duke and an Elvis impersonator. They introduced me as a relationship expert and after joking around about bad dates, Trixy said, "Why would you write a book on relationships anyhow?"

"After losing money in the stock market several years ago, I went on a spiritual retreat and God called me to write about the most valuable lessons in life."

"Now we have heard it all, ladies and gentlemen! Not only does God exist, but God actually talks to people. Isn't that just the wackiest thing you have ever heard?" Duke said.

"Hey," the Elvis impersonator cut in, "I talk to my Stradacaster all the time. But it never talks back, HA HA HA!"

After they laughed hysterically for over a minute, they cut me off. The phone line went dead and deeply wounded my soul. I didn't even have a chance to get a word in edgewise. They took what was sacred and turned it into a big joke.

After fighting off the shame of personal rejection, I was faced with another difficult decision. Should I talk about God and run the risk of offending people, or should I play along with the interview and try to sell books?

If sex, smut and trash sells books and keeps the audience interested, should I go along with it or follow the teaching from Matthew 6:24? *No one can serve two masters; for a slave will either hate the one and love the other, or be devoted to the one and despise the other. You cannot serve God and wealth.*

I had already learned that lesson once when I lost a quarter million dollars trading commodities. The Lord was lord of my life, and I decided to take a stand for God. I didn't care if it made secular radio hosts uncomfortable. Not only was I going to talk about God, but also Jesus Christ, His only begotten Son.

I started praying before every interview and as I felt led by the Spirit, I would mention my belief in Jesus. The name alone seemed to break any negativity or lack of respect coming over the air waves. I focused my interviews on the message of personal healing and put my trust in God concerning the book sales.

After all, Matthew 10:32 says, *Everyone therefore who acknowledges me before others, I also will acknowledge before my Father in heaven; but whoever denies me before others, I also will deny before my Father in heaven.*

After Valentine's Day I did a few interviews that focused on the aftermath of the romantic holiday. I gave books out to callers and was able to offer practical advice and encouragement to those who felt let down by their partners. It brought me great joy to minister to others in need. Afterwards, I decided to keep the radio shows going for another couple months.

The P.R. firm had stopped booking shows, so I bought a list of radio stations and started making calls myself. I spoke to producers, sent out review copies, and tried to tie the interview questions into the latest news trends. It took a while to get a pipeline of shows scheduled, but eventually I was doing several interviews a day.

As I worked my way through the list, I came across a local AM talk station with the call letters 1090-PUKE. Most of my interviews were with out-of-state stations, so when I found a possible in-studio opportunity, I jumped at the chance to meet the host and producers personally. I wanted to establish an ongoing relationship and be a regular guest on their show.

As I drove to the station I tuned in and listened to a couple of guys talking about a new baseball tax and how they didn't like the bathroom stalls in the new stadium. I figured their show could use some help and walked into the downtown office building feeling confident and secure. After stepping off the elevator on the seventeenth floor, I proceeded through two glass doors and greeted the receptionist with a smile. She was working the phones and in between calls she said, "Can I help you?"

"I'm here to see a producer for your afternoon show."

"Hold on, I'll see if she's available."

As I took a seat in a gray chair, the receptionist paged the producer and relayed my request. Suddenly we were involved in a three-way conversation as the receptionist talked back and forth between me and the producer.

"Do you have an appointment?" she asked.

"Nope, just dropped in."

"He doesn't have an appointment!" she said.

After a brief pause in the conversation the receptionist said good-bye to the producer and started taking other calls. People continued walking in and out of the office and talking to her while I waited. I assumed someone would be out to see me momentarily, but after I waited fifteen minutes, the receptionist looked up and said, "Our producer's very busy, you can leave your information."

Why didn't she tell me sooner? I thought as I handed her my book and stomped out of the office.

Later that afternoon I received a call from the producer's assistant, wanting to know if I was available for a 3 p.m. interview. "Sure!" I said, overjoyed.

The station called on time, and several minutes into the interview the host interrupted me and said, "Do you know why you're being interviewed today?"

"To discuss relationships?" I offered.

"You threw your book at me!" A voice screeched in

the background.

"Here you are, Mr. Relationship Repair Man, and this is how you treat our receptionist? She's the sweetest girl alive, and you stomp into our office and demand to see our very busy producer. Then you have the nerve to get mean and nasty and throw your book at her, because you had to wait a few minutes! How dare you?"

"I handed it to her. I'm sorry for my attitude, but she disrespected me by making me wait fifteen minutes before telling me the producer wasn't available."

I tried to explain my side of the story, but the host cut me off and started taking callers. I ran to the radio to listen, and the first caller was on my side. He was a business owner who said, "In my office, it's the receptionist's job to make everyone feel welcome." After that, it got very ugly.

The callers started bashing me with the foulest, most abusive language I have ever encountered, and the host kept reiterating distorted information.

I should have done my homework. I didn't realize 1090-PUKE was a slash and bash talk station, though by the call letters, I should have suspected something. They criticized everyone and everything. I had been set up, and felt sick to my stomach.

Immediately, I started to pray and could feel the Lord's protection surrounding my heart. It was like a peaceful shield of comfort and reassurance that I could physically feel every time I turned the radio on to hear what was happening.

They made fun of my book and twisted sentences out of context, and everyone laughed as they called me filthy names. I wanted to call back and be very loving and nice. I wanted to take a stand for righteousness and tell them about my critical father and how the healing process is available to everyone. It was the perfect audience for my message, but I was outnumbered and overpowered. They carried the topic to its bitter end. It lasted more than three hours.

Eleven

⮜⭕✝⭕⮞

$\mathcal{A}$s the months passed, my relationship with God continued to grow. I was praying more and during the hard times of persecution, I learned to depend on the Lord for my very existence and survival. I discovered a sweet intimacy when I ran to Jesus for protection. Just knowing He was close at hand gave me more courage to boldly proclaim His message as the radio shows and healing seminars continued.

Cindy was a great support and encouragement to me during this time. Our friendship continued to grow, and every time we got together, our conversation turned towards the Christian walk. I couldn't wait to see her again.

Earlier in the week we made plans for a lunch date at her favorite restaurant — The Sushi Garden. As I arrived, she was standing out front. I held the door open for her, and after our waiter seated us at a small table in the corner, she leaned forward and said, "Share with me your heart."

"What do you mean?"

"You never open up. We talk about other people's lives, current events, even deep spiritual concepts, but you never share the depths of your heart with me."

"Say what?"

"My other friends trust me enough to spill their guts. Everyone goes through hard times. If something's bothering you, I want to know. I'll be there for you."

After our food arrived, Cindy kept directing pointed questions into my heart. They felt Spirit-led, because after a while I broke down. All the negative emotions I had repressed in an attempt to be positive were now coming to the surface.

"I have spent years making sure every word was perfect. I tried everything — public speaking, radio shows, direct mail, trade shows, book signings, advertising, and nothing seems to work. It's impossible to make money. Plus all the abuse I'm suffering. It's like I made God a Father's Day card, and He crumpled it up and threw it in the trash!"

"Do you feel better now?"

"No, I hate feeling like this."

Cindy looked like she was going to start crying herself. I could feel her care and concern staring at me through her radiant blue eyes. "Let's go outside and pray," she said, getting up to leave.

We walked to a nearby park and sat down in the grass across from a waterfall that overflowed into a small pond. As I watched a little boy feeding the ducks in the distance, Cindy took a small Bible from her purse and read a quote from Ezekiel 36:25-26.

I will sprinkle clean water upon you, and you shall be clean from all your uncleannesses, and from all your idols I will cleanse you. A new heart I will give you, and a new spirit I will put within you; and I will remove from your body the heart of stone and give you a heart of flesh.

"Do you see how important the heart is to God?" Cindy asked. "In the Old Covenant, God commanded the Israelites to keep hundreds of purification rituals because He wanted to dwell among them. In the New Covenant, God still requires holiness, but now He wants to dwell in our hearts. I will remove your heart of stone and give you heart of love alone.

"Jesus didn't come to abolish the Law and the prophets, He came and expanded upon them to incorporate our hearts, minds and attitudes. Jesus requires internal holiness, because He wants to dwell inside our hearts.

"The divine presence of God cannot dwell when we're full of anger, bitterness, resentment and greed of money. It's not what enters the mouth that defiles a man, but the evil intentions from within the heart."

"I am full of anger, but I don't know what to do."

"You need to dig down and surrender your hurt and resentment. Holding on to it only hinders God and harms you. Cry out to your Father, so that He can start working on the situation."

Digging deep in my heart, I began to pray like never before. I vented all my frustration and disappointment for what seemed like an hour, and afterwards I was exhausted. It was then I realized the difference between head prayers and heart prayers. I had been saying words with my mouth, *Lord, I give you my life and book sales, let it be done according to your will.* But my heart told a different story. It was full of venomous hurt.

In a way, I wasn't being truthful with God. I wasn't worshipping or serving the Father in spirit or truth like the quote from John 4:23-24 spoke about. *...the hour is coming, and is now here, when the true worshipers will worship the Father in spirit and truth, for the Father seeks such as these to worship him. God is spirit, and those who worship him must worship in spirit and truth.*

As Cindy and I left the park that evening, I felt much better. I had given my hurt and pain to the Lord and could now surrender book sales into His hands. Even if my financial situation didn't change, at least I was being straight with God.

For the next several weeks, I continued thinking about the mechanics of the heart. The words of Ezekiel kept replaying over and over again in my mind. *A new heart I will give you, and a new spirit I will put within you.* I didn't fully understand the quote until I received an urgent message from Cindy one morning.

"You won't believe what happened," she said. "The Lord gave me a vision about you. It was so beautiful, I couldn't stop crying."

"I'll be right over," I said.

Cindy's condominium complex was located ten minutes away, and as I pulled in front of her three-story building, she ran outside to greet me. "Let's sit in the shade, there's a gazebo over here."

As I followed her towards the white latticework structure that was surrounded by flowers in the center of the courtyard, she started describing the vision. "You were being baptized by Jesus. At first, He immersed you in water, but only a part of your face went under.

72

Then He immersed you a second time, and your entire body went under. When you came up, a childlike radiant joy flowed from your presence. The emotions were so powerful they made me weep."

"What do you think it means?"

"I don't know, but I can still feel the radiant joy."

"I don't think the meaning can be taken literally, because I've already been baptized twice."

"What do you mean?" she asked.

"When I started doing healing seminars at New Life Church, the pastor wanted me to get baptized a second time. He said, Jesus was completely immersed in water as an adult and so should His followers. I didn't feel led by the Spirit but I did it anyway, just to make him happy.

"Nothing happened to me spiritually, so there has to be another meaning to the vision. Like maybe the book. Maybe the second reprint is going to shine with that radiant joy you were describing?"

"Let's pray about it. If we continue seeking, He will show you the answers."

Twelve

❦

Several weeks later, I continued to petition the Lord for the meaning of Cindy's vision. I was sure it had something to do with my book. I was working on a second edition in hopes that some minor revision would increase sales. The work was going great, until one day, when I had an uncomfortable feeling deep in my heart.

I sat down to pray in the corner of my room, next to a black pot containing a large ficus tree. I could feel something negative stirring deep within. At first, I wanted to distract myself from the uncomfortable feelings, but instead, I decided to embrace whatever it was head-on.

After a lot of prayer, the Lord showed me a vision of my heart. It looked like a piece of gray metal and had a tiny metal door that opened and closed almost like a door on a matchbox car.

Compared to God's radiant splendor my heart was empty and lifeless because I had never invited Jesus inside. I never allowed the Lover of my soul complete access to the most sacred part of my being.

Sure, I said the words a million times, *Lord Jesus, I give you my life and heart;* but in the moment of truth, I realized I had been withholding my heart. I had surrendered my business life to the Lord and was working in full-time ministry, but I'd never allowed Jesus inside.

Returning to the vision, I pictured the gray metal door opening wide, as I offered an invitation for Jesus to come inside.

It didn't work. Nothing happened, and I started getting scared.

Immediately, I called Cindy and said, "Do you remember that vision you had about me being baptized twice? Well, I have never given Jesus my heart."

"Wow, that's serious! Do you want to pray about it?"

"I'll leave right away."

Upon arriving, I slowly made my way up the wooden stairwell to the third floor. Cindy's door was open, so I announced my presence and walked inside and sat down in her rocking chair.

"You look sad," she said, as she came over to give me a hug.

"I can't believe Jesus wouldn't honor my request. I invited Him inside. What do you think's wrong?"

"Have you totally committed everything? Jesus wants to dwell inside everyone's heart, but good and evil don't mix. Your motives need to be pure and true. Your spiritual house needs to be swept clean, totally sold out to God's will for your life."

"I'm sinless! Except for little things every now and then. And emotional baggage, I have spent years healing every minute detail."

"I know how hard you've worked, but there has to be something holding you back. Are you willing to have your life turned upside down? Can Jesus violate your free will and do anything He wants with you?"

"Wait a second, what do you mean, *anything*?"

"If Jesus called you to live as a celibate monk in Africa, would you go?"

"Jesus wouldn't say that to me!"

"It doesn't matter, once you come to a place of complete surrender, you'll do anything to please the Lord. To the rich young ruler, Jesus said, go sell everything and give the money to the poor. Then come and follow me. The cost of discipleship is extremely high. In Luke 14:25-35 Jesus describes the requirements like this.

Now large crowds were traveling with him; and he turned and said to them, "Whoever comes to me and does not hate father and mother, wife and children, brothers and sisters, yes, and even life itself, cannot be my disciple. Whoever does not carry the cross and follow me cannot be my disciple. For which of you, intending to build a tower, does not first sit down and estimate the cost, to see whether he has enough to complete it? Otherwise, when he has laid a foundation and is not able to finish, all who see it will begin to ridicule him, saying, 'This fellow began to build and was not able to finish.' Or what king, going out to wage war against another king, will not sit down first and consider whether he is able with ten thousand to oppose the one who comes against him with twenty thousand? If he cannot, then, while the other is still far away, he sends a delegation and asks for the terms of peace. So therefore, none of you can become my disciple if you do not give up all your possessions.

"The cost of discipleship is extremely high," Cindy

said again. "You are required to love God with your entire heart, mind, body and soul and put nothing before Him."

"You're right! I have spent a lot of time constructing my spiritual tower, and I'm not going to stop short. I want to give Jesus my heart, and I don't care what He does with my life afterwards!"

"Do you want to pray now?" Cindy asked.

"No, I can't invite the God of the universe into my heart from your living room. You have an electric fan blowing in the corner. I want a mountaintop experience. Let's drive to the highest summit we can find, and from there, I'll cry out to God with complete surrender."

"Sounds great, give me a few minutes to get ready."

As Cindy drove her Jeep up Highway 285 towards the mountains, I looked out the window at the towering forest evergreens that consumed the steep hillside with their rugged beauty. As I noticed the flowing stream alongside the road and the gentle leaves of the aspen trees blowing in the wind, I could sense something big was about to happen.

We arrived at Lookout Point just before sunset. The sky was painted with a thousand different shades of pink and orange, and I could see the sparkling city lights below. It was the perfect location.

After climbing a rock formation on the southern side of the mountain, we sat in silence for a long time.

"How does this work?" I asked.

"Have you ever given your heart to a woman and

been head over heels in love?"

"A couple of times."

"It works the same way. When I gave my heart to Jesus, it was like falling in love with a romantic lover. You either allow yourself to fall in love and make yourself totally vulnerable and exposed, or you withhold your heart for whatever reason. I have fallen in love several times, and once I give my heart, it's all over. I'm totally committed.

"Falling in love with Jesus is the most exciting and passionate experience you'll ever encounter. Unlike romantic relationships, Jesus will never hurt you or let you down."

"That makes sense. I have dated women for months and never given my heart. In fact, I could probably marry a woman and give her all of my time and money, and never let her inside. I guess that's what I have been doing to Jesus."

"It happens all the time, but it's not a true marriage," Cindy said.

As the evening twilight slowly faded into the night, I begged Jesus to enter my heart. I surrendered everything to Him, my life, heart, body, mind, intellect and free will. I reached down deep inside and totally exposed my soul.

Afterwards I had a peaceful, warm glow. I could feel a difference in my spirit as we drove home that evening.

The next day I couldn't wait to tell Cindy what happened. Running to the phone I called her and said,

"It worked! Jesus entered my heart, and I can actually feel His presence. He has been traveling around with me ever since."

"I can hear the difference in your voice."

"I feel different too, especially when I pray. Before, it felt like my words hit the top of my head and stopped. Like God was up in Heaven and a huge void separated my prayers from Jesus. Now that I'm carrying His presence around in my heart, it feels like I'm praying directly with Him.

"And the words *I love you* take on a whole new meaning. I used to say them all the time, but now, I can actually feel my love for Jesus."

"I'm so happy for you!" Cindy said. "I know when I had my spiritual awakening things changed dramatically. My religious behaviors transformed from a rote routine into a passionate, heartfelt relationship. My encounter with Jesus happened a little different from yours, but once it did, I was on fire for the Lord. My evangelist efforts took off."

"What do you mean?"

"I prayed to God for many years before inviting Jesus into my heart. I believed in Jesus, but it was my own personal belief, and I felt uncomfortable sharing my views with others. After surrendering my heart, something inside me changed. I became spirit-filled and couldn't stop talking about the Lord. It changed my life. I'm excited to see what's going to happen to you."

"Yeah, me too. My Bible study group needs to hear this message. I can't wait to tell them what happened.

Everyone needs a spirit-filled conversion experience."

"I'll keep your group in my prayers," Cindy said as we got off the phone.

Thirteen

❧ ✝ ❧

During the rest of the week my emotions were flooded with the peaceful presence of Christ — Himself. Before I surrendered everything, I had to pray for hours to reach these deep levels of sweetness and peace. Now, several minutes into my prayer time, the euphoric feelings overwhelmed me. It was like Jesus had taken residence deep within my heart and followed me around wherever I went.

I noticed the biggest difference one evening driving over to Scott's house for group. I was running late and flying down the highway in my black Corvette. Cutting in and out of traffic, I was passing cars like they were standing still.

It felt like Jesus was riding with me in the passenger seat. His presence was so strong I could feel His disapproval. "But Lord," I said, "I always drive like this. Lighten up, I'm sure you'll get used to it."

I arrived at Scott's house a few minutes late, and after Becky finished describing her prayer request, I said, "You guys are never going to guess what happened."

"Lord of your life?" Scott said sarcastically.

"Nope, Captain of the heart."

After I described Cindy's vision and my mountain-top conversion experience, Joann cut me off and said, "That sounds New Age."

"It's totally from God. Just look at Romans 10:9-10: *because if you confess with your lips that Jesus is Lord and believe in your heart that God raised him from the dead, you will be saved. For one believes with the heart and so is justified, and one confesses with the mouth and so is saved.*

"Before my conversion experience, I did a lot of confessing with my mouth, but I didn't have the ability to believe with my heart, until I surrendered my heart. Once I healed my emotional baggage and surrendered my free will, Jesus entered my heart and gave me the ability to believe with my heart.

"1 John 5:10-12 says the same thing. *Those who believe in the Son of God have the testimony in their hearts. Those who do not believe in God have made him a liar by not believing in the testimony that God has given concerning his Son. And this is the testimony: God gave us eternal life, and this life is in his Son. Whoever has the Son has life; whoever does not have the Son of God does not have life.*

"I have been doing a lot of religious behaviors and have withheld my heart from Jesus all these years out of fear. It's only by the grace of God that He called me into a spirit-filled personal relationship."

"It still sounds New Age," Joann said. "Don't you know about the Angel of Light? Satan disguises himself in ways that look good on the outside. Then by the time you're deceived, it's too late."

"That's why I'm concerned for you guys," I said. "If I never gave Him my heart until now, I wonder how many other Christians haven't either. Are you sure you have the testimony of Jesus dwelling in your hearts?"

"Where do you get off?" Scott asked. "We're all saved Christians who love the Lord, or else we wouldn't be here. If you love the Lord so much, why aren't you here every week?"

"Because I'm sick of arguing. I came to deliver a serious message..."

"And we're sick of your distractions," Scott said.

"If that's what you think, I'm leaving."

"Go ahead!"

After stomping out of Scott's house in anger, I began to pray on my way home. "I'm sorry, Lord, please forgive me. I shouldn't have blown it like that. I just wanted to share the message, but it's like they don't care. They don't want to know you deeper, and it grieves me tremendously."

The next day, my feelings of conviction continued. I called Scott and apologized, although I had little desire to return to his group. I mostly wanted the peaceful feeling from my conversion experience to return. It slowly faded away when I left Scott's house, and I would do anything to get it back.

The long dry spell continued for more than a week, until one day I realized the problem driving home from work. The Lord had told me to slow down many times, but I didn't listen. Now, it felt like He wanted me to drive the speed limit. I set the cruise control, and almost instantly, His peaceful presence came rushing back. My spiritual rut ended, and I was overjoyed.

The only problem was, a huge line of cars began backing up behind me. Most people on the highway travel ten to fifteen miles per hour over the speed limit, and soon impatient motorists started swarming around me.

I tried to stay in the slow lane and fight the urge to speed, but it was just too humbling. I liked the adrenaline rush of ruling the road and racing other cars off the line. Over time, my driving commitment to the Lord slowly faded away.

Not long after, I started experiencing another dry time. I felt like a parched desert in need of life-giving water, so on Cindy's recommendation, I made an appointment with her spiritual director — Dr. Patterson. Her office was located in a white high-rise office building on the other side of town.

As I arrived for my appointment, I could feel the tension rising as the elevator carried me to the sixteenth floor. I was greeted by a middle-aged woman with long dark hair who said, "Hi, I'm Jill Patterson. Please have a seat."

Her office consisted of a large room with five rocking chairs and three couches, all arranged in a circle around a glass table. I took a seat across the room from a grandfather clock that stood majestically against a wall covered with academic degrees and several cases of books.

"How can I help you?" she asked in a soft voice.

"I need direction concerning a book project I'm working on. The Lord called me to write it several years ago, and now I feel stuck. I'm also suffering a terrible dry time. It feels like I took a wrong turn somewhere."

"I always pray for clients before they arrive, and the Lord wanted me to give you the second chapter of Proverbs. Why don't you read it and tell me what kind of emotions it brings forth."

After opening a Bible that was lying on the table in front of me, I read the text and said, "Nothing's jumping out at me."

"Why don't you read it again?"

"It's not going to help, I read Proverbs all the time. I need to hear from the Lord, not more Bible quotes."

"I can share hundreds of ways to draw closer to God, but right now, the Lord wants to speak through Proverbs. Why don't you call me after carefully meditating on each word?"

I left Patterson's office in anger. Why did I pay her $50 to read the second chapter of Proverbs? I wanted the peaceful presence of God to fill my heart, not to drive across town and get ripped off!

On my way home, I stopped at an old stone church in lower downtown Denver. As I entered the sanctuary, I could feel the peaceful presence of God inside. The gothic architecture, marble columns and stained glass windows produced a deep sense of reverence.

I took a seat near the altar and started praying. After about an hour, I opened my Bible to read Proverbs 2:1-5 again.

My child, if you accept my words and treasure up my commandments within you, making your ear attentive to wisdom and inclining your heart to understanding; if you indeed cry out for insight, and raise your voice for understanding; if you seek it like silver, and search for it as for hidden treasures — then you will understand the fear of the Lord and find the knowledge of God.

After reading it over and over, I started getting mad at God. "What do you mean, if I treasure up your commandments? I have kept them! I have given you everything. I'm working for nothing. I have given you my heart, my livelihood, my everything. What else do you want?"

Then after humbling myself before the Lord God Almighty I asked, "What commandments haven't been kept?"

Like of a flash of lightning, the Lord showed me a vision. I was in the passenger seat of my black Corvette, and Jesus was driving down the freeway. He looked over at me and said, "If you can't drive the speed limit, sell the car."

His words cut through me like a knife. Immediately, I left the pew and got down on the floor. With my face to the cold marble, I begged the Lord's forgiveness. Instantly, the Holy Spirit returned bringing a refreshing sensation of joy.

As I left the old stone church and drove home that day, I was bombarded with ruthless motorists who swarmed around me like angry bees. All I could do was watch my speedometer and pray. I felt exposed and vulnerable, almost like I was going to get stung at any moment for inconveniencing everyone else on the road.

Fourteen

The next day I called Dr. Patterson and set another appointment. I was lucky to get in and see her so quickly. Normally she scheduled several weeks out, but because one of her clients canceled, I was able to see her later that afternoon.

As I walked into her office a little after 2 p.m., I had many mixed feelings. I was overjoyed to have the peaceful presence of the Lord back, but was feeling burdened over the driving issue. "Why me?" I asked after telling the story.

"Because obedience is a biblical requirement for all who want to live a godly life in Jesus Christ," she said.

"Let me read you a quote from Romans 13:1. *Let every person be subject to the governing authorities; for there is no authority except from God, and those authorities that exist have been instituted by God.*

"Peter says the same thing in 1 Peter 2:13. *For the Lord's sake accept the authority of every human institution...*

"As Christians, we are required to follow all of man's laws so long as they don't conflict with God's laws. Traffic laws are designed to protect everyone, and when you intentionally violate them, not only are you endangering others, but you're also committing sin."

"Speeding's not a sin!"

"If the Bible requires you to be obedient to the governing authorities and human institutions set up for the protection of your fellow brothers and sisters, and you intentionally violate these laws and justify the behavior in your own mind, then yes, I call that sin."

"But Jesus died on the cross for my sins. Everyone sins, that's why we need a Savior."

I was expecting to get into a theological argument with Dr. Patterson, but she just looked at me with piercing eyes. The chair where I was sitting became very uncomfortable and she finally broke the long silence by reading a quote from Matthew 5:48. *Be perfect, therefore, as your heavenly Father is perfect.*

"Peter also makes this point clear in 1 Peter 1:14-16. *Like obedient children, do not be conformed to the desires that you formerly had in ignorance. Instead, as he who called you is holy, be holy yourselves in all your conduct; for it is written, "You shall be holy, for I am holy."*

"How's that possible?" I asked.

Flipping through the pages of her Bible, she responded by saying, "Hebrews 12:4: *In your struggle against sin you have not yet resisted to the point of shedding your blood.*"

"You're right, but isn't that kind of harsh?"

"In the Old Testament, the penalty for sin was death. When an Israelite committed a major sin, the elders convened and brought forth witnesses. If the violator of the law was found guilty, he was pelted with rocks until he died. When someone committed a minor sin, the penalty was still death, but he was allowed to sacrifice the life of a sheep or goat in place of his own. The animal's blood was sprinkled upon the altar, fulfilling the law of Moses and making the necessary atonement.

"Today the penalty for sin is still death. The God of the Old Testament is also the God of the New Testament. Instead of sacrificing animals every year, Jesus was slaughtered once and for all in their place. Now we can confess our sins to Jesus, the Sacrificial Lamb, and ask His blood to wash us clean.

"That doesn't mean we can sin all we want and expect to be forgiven because Hebrews 10:26-29 contains serious consequences for those who call themselves Christian and continue to live in their sinfulness:

For if we willfully persist in sin after having received the knowledge of the truth, there no longer remains a sacrifice for sins, but a fearful prospect of judgment, and a fury of fire that will consume the adversaries. Anyone who has violated the law of Moses dies without mercy 'on the testimony of two or three witnesses.' How much worse punishment do you think will be deserved by those who have spurned the Son of God, profaned the blood of the covenant by which they were sanctified, and outraged the Spirit of grace?"

"What about Romans 8:39?" I asked. *"Nothing can separate me from the love of God."*

"Taken in context, that quote is very beautiful. Paul is talking about obedient, God-fearing disciples who are walking the walk and experiencing hardships, distress and persecution. If you're truly God's child, then yes, nothing can separate you from His love.

"But don't think for a second that sin and worldly vanities will not separate you from God, because 1 John 2:15 says: *Do not love the world or the things in the world. The love of the Father is not in those who love the world.*

"It's important to understand the two different classes of people of which the Bible speaks. There are God's children and the Babylonian enemies, who were destroyed. The weeds and the wheat, the sheep and the goats, the lost children from the house of Israel and the dogs who take away their food.

"God's children act in ways that bring glory to the Father, and the children of destruction seek after their worldly and fleshly concerns."

"I thought we were all God's children," I said.

"We are all God's creation, but not everybody is God's child. 1 John 3:10 says: *The children of God and the children of the devil are revealed in this way: all who do not do what is right are not from God...* Anyone can call himself a Christian, but it doesn't mean he's walking a godly walk or being an obedient child."

"What should I do about my friends?"

"What do you mean?"

"I have been going to a Bible study group where everyone sits around giving their own rendition of sacred scripture. Becky, a recent convert from the New Age movement, always puts a universal Mother Earth slant on her text. Scott, a conservative fundamentalist, tries to persuade everyone to his point of view. Their lives are full of sin, and after the weekly debate, everyone leaves thinking it's OK to decipher the word of God any way they want."

"It's not your place to pass judgment. You're here to work on your own issues. Don't get sidetracked. Stay focused on Christ and His will for your life.

"If Jesus says, drive the speed limit, you have to make a choice. You can choose to glorify your Father or justify your sinful behavior."

"How come you're taking such a hard stance? I thought we were saved by faith, not by sinless conduct."

"Because in Revelation 3:1-6, John was sent to deliver a message to the newly established church in Sardis. His message to the Christian community was simple — if they didn't change their ways and repent, their names would be stricken from the book of life.

...I know your works; you have a name of being alive, but you are dead. Wake up, and strengthen what remains and is on the point of death, for I have not found your works perfect in the sight of my God. Remember then what you received and heard; obey it, and repent. If you do not wake up, I will come like a thief, and you will not know at what hour I will come to you. Yet you have still a few persons in Sardis who have not soiled their clothes; they will walk with me, dressed in white, for they are worthy. If you conquer, you will be clothed like them in white robes, and I will not blot your name out of the book of life; I will confess your name before my Father and before his angels. Let anyone who has an ear listen to what the Spirit is saying to the churches.

"There's no difference between the Christian church located in Sardis and our modern-day Christian churches. If we do not wake up, obey the word of God, repent of our sinfulness and reform our lives, it's possible to have our names blotted out of the book of life.

"Do you know what that means?" she asked.

"If your name's not found in the book, you're not getting in?"

"Exactly. Revelation 20:12-15 defines it as follows: *...another book was opened, the book of life. And the dead were judged according to their works, as recorded in the books. And the sea gave up the dead that were in it, Death and Hades gave up the dead that were in them, and all were judged according to what they had done. Then Death and Hades were thrown into the lake of fire. This is the second death, the lake of fire; and anyone whose name was not found written in the book of life was thrown into the lake of fire."*

Looking down at her watch, Dr. Patterson said, "For your homework this week, I want you to start examining your conscience every day. Take ten minutes and ask the Spirit to disclose all your shortcomings. After you feel a true conviction of heart, make your amends to God and vow some type of reform.

"I also want you to do a word search on Galatians 5:19-21: *Now the works of the flesh are obvious: fornication, impurity, licentiousness, idolatry, sorcery, enmities, strife, jealousy, anger, quarrels, dissensions, factions, envy, drunkenness, carousing, and things like these. I am warning you, as I warned you before: those who do such things will not inherit the kingdom of God.*

"Do you know what *licentiousness* means?" she asked.

"Not really."

"If you're serious about inheriting the kingdom, you might want to look it up."

"I'll do that. Thanks again doc, see ya next week."

Fifteen

Over the next several months, I continued working on my sinful nature. Every time I examined my conscience, I would find something to confess and work on the next day. Looking at my shortcomings was unpleasant, but every time I repented with a sorrowful heart, I experienced more of the Lord's peaceful presence.

My biggest battle of sin to overcome was impatient driving. Every time I looked at the speedometer, I had to slow down and remind myself how much I loved the Lord's laws. I practically invented road rage, and the only way I could drive the speed limit was to remain in constant prayer. I thought I had the situation under control, until one day when a man cut me off.

I was traveling southbound on Highway 225 and could see a white vehicle approaching quickly in my rearview mirror. It was a late-model Camero, and as the driver flew past, his car kicked up a rock that chipped my windshield.

I was outraged! I fought with all my might to stay peaceful, but my rage was too strong. I slammed the accelerator to the floor and within seconds, I was closing in at speeds well over a hundred miles per hour. I wanted to cut him off so bad I could taste it, but before

I could catch him, he took the next exit.

Eventually my fury wore off and I slowed down. I felt terrible. I wanted to please the Lord, but didn't have the power.

Later that week, I told Dr. Patterson what happened. She taught me about the workings of evil and how to stand strong by putting on the full armor of God. The spiritual warfare prayers she gave me helped control the negative spirit that came over me, but I had to struggle for many more months before the Lord set me free.

It happened on my way to a very important meeting. Traffic was light, I had the cruise control set at 58 miles per hour and cars were flying past me on both sides. I kept looking at the clock, counting how many minutes I would be late.

The tension about being late was killing me, so I started passing cars. After a while my guilt started flaring up, so I slowed back down. It felt like I was stuck between a rock and a hard place, with no other option, except to suffer.

Eventually, I broke down and started pounding on the steering wheel. "Lord, I can't take this anymore!" I felt so pathetic before Him. He had given me one simple assignment, and I had let Him down. I didn't have the strength.

In my brokenness and shame, I finally surrendered.

I gave Him my inability, and as I did, something inside of me changed. I didn't realize it at first, but the Lord delivered me and gave me complete peace. It was a night-and-day difference. For the first time in my life, I didn't care if everyone on the road raced past me. I now had the peace of Christ traveling with me. I had acquired the ability to drive across town in the worst possible traffic conditions and still remain spirit-filled.

Overjoyed, I told Dr. Patterson what happened at our next appointment.

"Congratulations," she said. "That's a beautiful example of Christ's purpose. Jesus didn't come to cover over our sins with His good name. He came to dwell in our hearts and bring us the internal strength to overcome our sinful nature."

"I never knew that."

"As Christians, we are required to be holy as God is holy, but unfortunately no one has that strength or ability on his own. It's only by inviting the presence of Christ into our lives that we obtain the power to stand victorious over our sinful nature.

"Several months ago God gave you a formidable challenge of driving the speed limit. He knew about your pride and control issues. He also wanted to stretch and test your abilities of obedience. After you passed the test and surrendered your weaknesses, Jesus gave you the power to overcome that area of sin in your life.

"I call it the Journey of Endurance, because through your sincere effort and constant struggle, Christ honored your request. If you never fought the battle, you would never have obtained the victory."

"Great," I said. "But now that my driving's under control, I still need direction on my book project."

"Maybe the Lord wanted to remove sin from your life first. If you're unwilling to obey a simple command, why should He give you extra revelation or special assignments?"

"Good point. Now that I'm walking in obedience, let's talk about how to hear from the Lord. I feel stuck. Book sales are slow, I'm not making money. I have all kinds of abilities, and the Lord has me sitting around doing nothing."

"Since your hour is almost up, why don't we walk across the street for lunch? I don't usually eat with clients, but it will give us a chance to talk."

"Sounds great," I said, as Dr. Patterson grabbed her purse from the filing cabinet.

After stepping into the hall, she locked the office door and we proceeded towards the lobby. It was filled with a soft light that filtered through the bronze windows that enclosed the entire building.

As we walked across the street, Dr. Patterson continued, "Hearing from the Lord is easy. There are only three requirements — obedience, tenacity and testing the spirits. The Lord's not going to speak if you're unwilling to heed His voice."

"What voice?" I asked as we reached the sidewalk.

Taking a small Bible from her purse, Dr. Patterson read a quote from John 10:3-9 & 27: *The gatekeeper opens the gate for him, and the sheep hear his voice. He calls his own sheep by name and leads them out. When he has brought out all his own, he goes ahead of them, and the sheep follow him because they know his voice. They will not follow a stranger, but they will run from him because they do not know the voice of strangers. Jesus used this figure of speech with them, but they did not understand what he was saying to them. So again Jesus said to them, 'Very truly, I tell you, I am the gate for the sheep. All who came before me are thieves and bandits; but the sheep did not listen to them. I am the gate. Whoever enters by me will be saved, and will come in and go out and find pasture. My sheep hear my voice, I know them, and they follow me.'*

"Are you listening for the Good Shepherd's voice?" she asked.

"Not really."

"Why not? Are you one of His sheep?"

"I am."

"Then why don't you know His voice?"

As we arrived at the Italian deli across the street from her office, I opened the door for Dr. Patterson. It looked to be a small mom-and-pop establishment, which was amazingly busy. We had to stand in line several minutes before ordering, but it gave us time to read a blackboard with brightly colored menu options.

It was possible to create your own pasta dish, so I ordered white sauce fettuccine with chicken, capers, artichoke hearts and pine nuts. After Dr. Patterson ordered an antipasto salad, we took a seat outside at a table with a large umbrella.

"I think I have the obedience part down. Tell me about tenacity," I said.

"That would be the relentless pursuit of God at any cost. Namely, prayer and fasting."

"I'm already doing a lot of prayer, but why should I starve myself for God?"

"Fasting is not about self-punishment. It's about going after God with everything you've got. Fasting puts the pursuit of God above your own physical needs for comfort and hunger. When you fast, your desire to hear God's voice becomes more important than your desire for food."

As we continued our conversation, a waiter arrived, carrying a large tray. He set our order, a pitcher of ice water and two glasses down on the table. It looked so good, I couldn't wait to eat. I looked up at Dr. Patterson to see if she wanted to say grace, but she just stared at me with that look again.

"What?" I asked.

"This is a perfect example for fasting. Can you feel your desire to eat right now?"

"Yeah, I'm starving."

"What's stronger, your desire to fill your soul with God, or the desire to fill your belly with carbohydrates? Do you have the strength to deny yourself and follow Jesus at any cost?"

"Not now, I'm starving."

"In Romans 8:5-8, Paul says: *For those who live according to the flesh set their minds on the things of the flesh, but those who live according to the Spirit set their minds on the things of the Spirit. To set the mind on the flesh is death, but to set the mind on the Spirit is life and peace. For this reason the mind that is set on the flesh is hostile to God; it does not submit to God's law — indeed it cannot, and those who are in the flesh cannot please God.*

"I used to overeat all the time," Dr. Patterson continued. "It was a false god, because I used food for emotional comfort instead of turning to the Lord. Once I started fasting, the Lord gave me the internal strength to break that area of bondage in my life."

"How do you fast?"

"On juice and water. I dedicate a certain number of days to the Lord and convert my hunger for food into a hunger for God and prayer."

"Days?" I asked.

"Jesus went forty days in the wilderness. Make a few protein shakes and drink lots of water. It won't hurt you. Your body can go weeks without food before it starts breaking down healthy tissue. Start small at first, by skipping a meal. Then work your way up to a full day. Once you get past the third day, you're on a spiritual high the rest of the week."

"Wow, that's hard-core."

She nodded. "For your homework, I want you to read the book of Daniel, and pray for God's will in your life concerning the process and discipline of fasting."

"I'll do it. Can we eat now?"

"Sure," she said, smiling.

Sixteen

The very next day, I decided to put breakfast off until noon. Instantly, I heard myself making whiny excuses. *I'm hypoglycemic. It will give me headaches. It will affect my health, and I'll lose too much weight.* After thinking about what was more important, the pursuit of God or my diet, I decided to give God a try.

I spent most of the morning in prayer, and the presence of the Lord was extremely strong. I could feel His loving warmth several times closer than usual. It felt like He was right beside me the entire time.

Before long, the morning had slipped away and it was time to break the fast with a bright red apple. The smell alone made my eyes water with pure excitement. I couldn't believe the amount of joy I was experiencing. It was so profound, I decided to go the next day without eating anything.

I started the morning with a lot of prayer, which helped me prepare for a 9 a.m. speaking engagement at the Rotary Club. My talk was well received, but afterwards, I found myself frustrated because traffic was at a standstill.

I started getting a headache and wanted to eat something to feel better. It was mostly mouth hunger, my stomach wasn't hungry. I just wanted to crunch on something sweet.

As traffic slowly moved forward, I noticed there was a bridge under construction ahead. All three lanes had to merge into a single line. A steady flow of cars kept passing everyone on the right shoulder, driving around the orange cones to cut in front of the line.

Just watching them made me irritable. I wanted to cut through the cones myself, but I took those thoughts captive and began to pray. I didn't feel like praying, but I cried out to the Lord with all my frustration and the strength of His spirit set me free.

It felt like evil was trying to sabotage my fasting efforts, so I made a decision to stand victorious and praise the Lord. I stayed in my own lane and prayed for the people who were cutting others off. I even let cars merge in front of me. The more I prayed, the stronger the Lord's presence grew. It was so powerful, I couldn't wait to tell Dr. Patterson at our next appointment.

"You'll never guess what happened," I said after walking into her office. "At first, I thought fasting was stupid, like, Why torture myself to please God? But it's not like that at all. God loves me so much that when I give up food for His sake, He feeds me supernaturally. It heightened my spiritual awareness and locked me into a constant state of prayer and praise all day."

"Congratulations! Now that you have experienced the presence of the Lord through fasting, you're ready for the discernment process."

"What's that like?" I asked.

"It starts with contemplative prayer. All you have to do is ask the Lord a question and listen for His answers. *Lord, what would you have me do today?* After sitting in silence and listening, for example, the Lord might show you an auditorium filled with people. If He does, ask Him, *What does this mean? Am I to set up another speaking engagement?*

"Or maybe the Lord will give you a feeling about another book or a counseling center to open. Just take it a piece at a time. Keep asking questions and make sure you discern and test the answers."

"Can you explain the listening part again?"

"Contemplative prayer works like a telephone call. When a friend calls, you don't talk nonstop for twenty minutes and then hang up the phone. Conversation needs to be two-sided. One person talks while the other listens.

"It works the same with God. Spend part of your prayer time pouring out petitions and the other part listening. It's like meditating on Jesus. When an intrusive thought enters your conscience, quickly dismiss it and refocus your attention back on Jesus. Like anything else, it's a discipline that will take time to master."

"It sounds easy, but why do I have to test the spirits?"

"Because it's a biblical directive, and also to make sure the information is coming from Jesus, not yourself or evil. There are three forces at work in the world — God, yourself and evil. When practicing contemplative prayer, it's your job to quiet your self-willed mind and listen to the voice of the Good Shepherd.

"The problem is that evil is sneaky. 1 Peter 5:8 says: *Discipline yourselves, keep alert. Like a roaring lion your adversary the devil prowls around, looking for someone to devour.*

"Evil is already at work in everybody's life so there's nothing to fear. You just need to recognize when evil is inserting thoughts into your mind and take them captive."

"How does that work?"

"Let's look at a compulsive gambler, for an example," she said. "After losing his wife, house and money, he wants to quit, but there's a spiritual force that keeps tempting and alluring him into sin. A tiny, whispering voice that says, *'Today's your lucky day. Go borrow more money and gain back all that you have lost.'*

"Because the gambler wants to quit, we know the voice is not coming from himself. We also know the voice is not coming from God. That only leaves one other option — evil."

"That happens to me all the time," I said. "Whenever I share my testimony or give a talk on emotional healing, a tiny whispering voice inside my head says, *'Your book's stupid, and you don't know what you're talking about.'* It really gets me discouraged, almost to the point of quitting."

"That would be evil, all right. It usually leaves us feeling angry, afraid, unfulfilled or tempted. Just be careful, because the voice of evil can also disguise itself in the form of something good. 2 Corinthians 11:14 says: *...Even Satan disguises himself as an angel of light.* Just because something sounds good doesn't mean it's from God."

"Can you explain that?"

"When Satan tempted Adam and Eve in the garden, he didn't say, 'Hi, I'm the devil, I'm here to destroy you. Please have some fruit.' Satan works by deceiving people and making the fruit look desirable. He says, *'If you eat it, you'll become like gods yourselves and gain the knowledge you desire.'*"

"How will I know? Let's say I ask Jesus a question, and I receive an answer in the form of an image. How do I know whether the message is from God or evil in disguise?"

"That's easy, 1 John 4:1-3 says: *Beloved, do not believe every spirit, but test the spirits to see whether they are from God; for many false prophets have gone out into the world. By this you know the Spirit of God: every spirit that confesses that Jesus Christ has come in the flesh is from God, and every spirit that does not confess Jesus is not from God. And this is the spirit of the antichrist, of which you have heard that it is coming; and now it is already in the world.*

"When you receive a message in contemplative prayer, all you need to do is ask the quiet stirring voice inside your heart, *'Can you confess that message as true before the Lord Jesus Christ of Nazareth who came in the flesh?'* If the message is from Jesus and the Bible tells you to test all spirits, then Jesus will give you some kind of confirmation."

"What if I test and don't get an answer?"

"If you seek the truth at all costs, you'll know the right answer. That's why fasting is an important part of the process. Don't start asking Jesus questions until you can feel His presence."

"Thanks, Dr. Patterson. I'll give it a try and let you know what happens."

Seventeen

After leaving Dr. Patterson's office, I drove to a white, gothic church by my house. It seemed like the perfect place to practice contemplative prayer, because of the quiet, serene atmosphere. The other churches in my neighborhood were closed during the week, but for some reason, St. Patrick's was always open.

As I entered the building, I could feel the presence of God. The sanctuary was filled with a soft, warm light, which filtered in through magnificent stained glass windows. From floor to ceiling, the towering glass arches displayed the life of Christ with breathtaking passion.

Because no one was around, I took my time walking down the aisle, trying to figure out the meaning behind each window. In one, the five water jars in the background and the newly married couple gave away the wedding feast at Canaan. In another, the terrified men on a small boat with a broken mast depicted Jesus walking on the water. The money exchangers being evicted, Lazarus emerging from the tomb, the woman at the well — all the major Gospel stories were displayed there in breathtaking beauty.

Taking a seat towards the front of the church, near a

marble statue of Jesus ascending into Heaven, I closed my eyes and tried to focus my attention on the Lord. During the first few minutes, all kinds of uncontrollable thoughts began racing around in my head. A list of things I forgot to do, memories from the past, day-dreams, even some negative judgments. I was excited at the prospect of hearing from the Lord, but couldn't quiet my mind to reach that tranquil place of stillness where it could happen.

After remembering Dr. Patterson's words, I changed my attitude and forced myself into silence. Whenever an intrusive thought entered my conscience, I quickly dismissed it and redirected my attention towards the Lord.

It helped to create a mental picture of Jesus. I imagined Him sitting directly in front of me and began looking deep into His eyes. Soon, I found myself overwhelmed by a sense of peace. I could feel the love of Christ touching my heart and soul. My breathing slowed down. It was just the Lord and me, gazing into each other's eyes.

It didn't seem appropriate to ask questions, so I just rested in His presence until the sound of a slamming door shattered my attention. People were starting to gather in the back of the church, and, looking at my watch, I couldn't believe the time. I had been in prayer for over an hour, and it only seemed like minutes. I didn't want to interrupt what looked to be a wedding rehearsal, so I quietly made my way towards an exit sign and slipped outside.

It was such a powerful experience, I went back the

next day with a list of questions. Once again the church was quiet and empty. Taking a seat in the same place, I started the process of quieting my mind. This time, it was a lot easier, except I found myself growing tired. I wanted to fall asleep, but instead, I took control of the situation and fired up my spirit.

Instead of being passive and allowing myself to drift off, I focused all of my energy and attention on the Lord. After longing after Him with all my might, I found that the distractions had disappeared and the peaceful presence of Christ had returned.

I wanted to ask the Lord some questions, but I couldn't stop thinking about a man from my past named Fred. He had borrowed a lot of money from me years ago and then declared bankruptcy. I thought I had forgiven him, but judging by the amount of anger that was boiling up inside me, I realized the Lord was prompting me to do more forgiveness work.

After asking God's assistance, I pictured an image of Jesus on the cross. He had nails driven through his hands and feet. His flesh was ripped open from being whipped, and a crown of thorns had been driven deep into His skull. Blood was running down His body and formed a large puddle on the ground where I was kneeling.

As I looked up into His tormented eyes, I imagined Fred entering the scene. He knelt down beside me. I turned to look at Fred, and seeing the tremendous amount of grief on his face made my heart break. For the first time in my life, I realized Fred hadn't intentionally hurt me. He had done the best he could and at the time, bankruptcy appeared to be his only option.

I was able to invite God's love into my hurt and surrender the debt to the Lord. After I did, God's love flooded in, bringing tears to my eyes. It was more than I could handle. I ended the imagination technique and walked out of the church with an overwhelming sense of peace and forgiveness in my heart.

The next day, I made a commitment to pray in silence every day for a year. Some days, the Lord's presence was crystal clear, and other times, I used all my strength to maintain total mental silence and never experienced anything.

Even though I was going to church every day and listening with all my strength, He still wasn't answering my prayers about my book. I kept asking the Lord how I needed to sell, advertise or distribute, but couldn't hear anything. Finally, in frustration I asked, *OK Lord. If you don't want me promoting the book anymore, what do you want me to do?*

As soon as I asked the question, a memory of a man I had met in San Diego came to mind. Even though I knew what the Lord wanted, I still tested the spirits to make sure the message could be confessed as true before the Lord Jesus Christ of Nazareth who came in the flesh.

After leaving the church I called Cindy and said, "You'll never guess what happened. Do you remember when I was on author tour in San Diego last year?"

"Sure," she said.

"At a gas station, I noticed a homeless man wandering around the middle of an intersection. He was begging for money, so after filling my tank, I called him over and gave him a few bucks. After talking with him, I found out he's a heroin addict and needed $40 a day to cover his withdrawal symptoms. He was caught in a deadly cycle, and it broke my heart to see him suffer.

"In my quiet time this morning, the Lord showed me the same guy in a vision. I could picture every detail of the gas station. The Lord didn't speak any words, but I know in my spirit that He wants me to live on the streets for a few days."

"Are you serious?" Cindy asked.

"Yeah, I'm serious. But why me?"

"The Lord probably wants to teach you something. Or maybe He's calling you into homeless ministry?"

"I hope not. You see them all over carrying beat-up signs: Will work for food."

"What are you going to do?"

"I'll keep praying about it."

Eighteen

To prepare for my upcoming weekend on the streets, I went to the thrift store for supplies. I couldn't picture myself pushing a shopping cart around, so I bought a green army duffel bag that could be converted into a backpack. I also bought a sleeping bag, just in case I couldn't get into a shelter.

Early Saturday morning, I dressed in an old pair of jeans, a gray sweat jacket with a hood and a green army trench coat. I also made several cardboard signs that read, 'Please help - sleeping under bridge tonight. Honk if you love Jesus. Need money for food.'

I left my cell phone and money at home and parked my truck at my parents' house, then walked to the nearest intersection. For over an hour, I held my sign and tried to make eye contact with people who were stopped at the red light, but no one would look at me. Everyone turned away or started looking for something on the floorboard of their car. When the light was green, people raced past me like I wasn't even there.

Eventually, their coldness and rejection found a way to my heart, and I sat down on the sidewalk with my head bent towards the ground. I couldn't take it anymore. It was going to be a long and painful weekend. I had given up all hope, when out of the corner of my eye, I spotted a red Toyota Corolla with two young children inside.

A little boy in the back seat was pointing at me, and the girl started waving. Their bright eyes and smiling faces filled me with joy. As I waved back, I caught their mother's attention, who by the reaction on the children's faces, was giving them a lecture about strangers. The little boy's countenance fell and he turned away from the window to look straight forward. The little girl stopped waving, but as the car drove away, she turned to smile at me one last time.

As I sat on the sidewalk thinking about what had happened, I realized people didn't want to acknowledge me because my situation might bring about a sense of conviction. If they ignored me, they could go about their daily routine without feeling obligated.

The thought grieved me because I had always been guilty of the same thing. I had put the pursuit of money and self-driven worldly agendas above my concern for people my entire life.

Looking up to the sky, I began to pray. *Well Lord, at least it's a beautiful day. Thanks for teaching me that lesson. I need help being more like you.*

Suddenly, my prayer was interrupted by a horn blaring and a woman yelling, "Do you need money?"

Jumping to my feet, I ran across the intersection towards her car and she handed me $6. I was overjoyed. I had just received all the money I needed to eat that day, and as she drove away, I prayed the Lord's blessings upon her.

It wasn't long before I caught the attention of a police officer. I could feel his disapproval staring at me through his mirrored sunglasses, so I grabbed my duffel bag and headed towards the bus stop.

After a short trip downtown, I wanted to see how my Honk if you love Jesus sign worked. I held it up for over an hour, and only one out of 100 cars sounded their horns. Most people who were stopped at the red light gave me dirty looks. Others laughed, and, judging by the expression on their faces, many took great offense.

Eventually, I put my sign away, and wandered away, grieved. I walked for a long time in the direction of the overnight shelter. Finally I came upon a group of homeless men standing in line for food. They were gathered in a parking lot around a pickup truck and several folding tables. I carefully studied the situation before summoning enough courage to join them for lunch.

After receiving a plate of sloppy joes, a doughnut and a glass of lemonade, I sat down next to a man and said. "So, what's your story?"

"I ain't got no story."

"Sorry, didn't mean to pry."

After a long period of silence I asked, "Who's serving lunch?"

"Some church group. You can have as much as you like. Go back for more."

"Thanks, but I feel kinda sick. Do you know anywhere to stay?"

"Here and there. When it's cold, I hang out on the hot air grates at 14th and Logan. Lately the cops have been busting everyone."

"What's up with the shelters?"

"Those stink holes! A bunch of snoring drunks, stinky feet, fist fights, no way. I would rather freeze to death outside."

As our conversation continued, I found out his name was Rex, and he gave me a list of feeding schedules and locations. He told me how I could make money working day labor, selling newspapers and panhandling. We even spoke about his drinking problem and how Jesus could deliver him if he was willing to surrender his life in complete obedience.

It turns out Rex had suffered a terribly abusive childhood. He was neglected by his mother, and his drunken stepfather always beat him bloody. Rex left home when he was eleven and started a life of drug and alcohol abuse. He had been in and out of jail, VA hospitals and living on the streets most of his life.

His story broke my heart. I wanted to help do anything. But what? Rex hadn't been inside a church in over ten years, but it brought him great joy when I asked his permission to pray for him every day for a month.

"You would do that for me?" he asked.

"Yes, I will! Jesus loves you, brother. Take care of yourself."

After talking to several more homeless men, I started walking towards the shelter to make sure I had a place to stay for the night. Any other day I would have used the sidewalk, but because of the way I was dressed, I kept to the alleyways.

The narrow passages between the buildings were littered with rubbish and vandalized with graffiti. The dumpsters were overflowing with trash, and the potholes were filled with murky water. The stench was terrible, but it was better than running into someone I knew along the way.

The shelter was located in a large, five-story red brick building on the corner of 23rd and Lawrence. It was surrounded by a black, wrought iron fence and posted with *No Loitering* signs every 100 feet. A security guard dressed in a navy blue uniform met me at the gate. I asked him if the shelter was open, and he said, "Sure. You'll need a TB card. Line up along the fence at 8 p.m., and we'll give you a mat on the floor for the night."

"What's a TB card?" I asked.

"Stands for tuberculosis. It's a highly contagious lung disease. The walk-in clinic will test you for free, but it takes three days to get the card."

"Three days!"

"The clinic's open from 12 to 2 on Tuesdays and Thursdays. When you show up for the test, they'll prick your arm with a vaccine. It takes twenty four hours to test the results. If the spot on your arm swells up, it means you're contagious. If you're clean, they'll issue a card the next day."

"I can't wait that long, I need a place tonight."

"Sorry, rules are rules," he shrugged and walked away.

After turning away discouraged, I took a seat underneath a tree across the street. As I continued to pray, I noticed a young woman who looked like she was in her early twenties walking towards me. She had long blonde hair tied back in a ponytail, and by the way she was dressed, I assumed she worked there. As she approach I said, "Excuse me. I don't have a TB card. Is there another shelter that can help me?"

"I'm here for a hotel voucher," she said. "They were supposed to have a lottery hours ago. When there's no room in the women's program, they give out free hotel rooms."

"Wow, a hotel room! That would be nice. Forgive me for asking, but why are you on the streets?"

"My boyfriend moved in with his parents, and they hate me. Last night we got into a huge fight, and they kicked me out."

"I'm sorry to hear that."

"Don't be, it happened all the time back in Indiana. What's up with you?"

"You won't believe me, but the Lord called me to live on the streets for a few days. I left everything behind — money, my car, a nice house. You probably think I'm a liar, but it's true."

"You own a house, and you're staying out here?"

"It's been a good adventure so far, but I need a place to stay for the night. I hate to ask, and it's not a sexual thing, but if you get a hotel voucher, would you mind if

I stayed with you? I'll sleep on the floor, nothing will happen."

"I don't even know if they'll give me one."

"Why don't you think about it? I'm going to run my sign in front of the church over there. If you get a voucher, come get me."

"I'll do that," she said.

Nineteen

$\mathcal{A}$s I approached the corner of 20th and California, I noticed a man with crutches sitting on the flower planters next to the church. By the way he was dressed, I figured he was homeless, so I sat down beside him and started talking. "What happened to your leg?"

"I passed out in the alley behind the liquor store. In the morning I was covered with snow. My toes were frozen. They didn't hurt but months later, I got real sick. The doctor at the hospital said it was gangrene, and he cut my leg off."

"That's harsh. I'm sorry. I can't believe no one helped you. Why didn't the owners of the liquor store do something? They just left you outside to freeze?"

"It happened to Vinny too. We used to ride freight trains together. It got too cold one night, and he died. I found him wrapped in a blanket, white as a ghost."

"How sad. What's going on now?"

"I'm waiting for service to get out. I need another pint."

Just then, the young woman I had met at the shelter walked up and sat down on the planter across from me. "My name's Gloria," she said, as the homeless man jumped up, grabbed his crutches and hopped towards the people who were exiting the church.

"They wouldn't give me a hotel voucher," she said. "I can't believe they made me sit outside for so long."

"What are you going to do?"

"I don't know."

"We could go down to the mall and run signs. Being a woman, I'd bet you'd make a ton of money. Then we could rent a room for the night."

"Won't we get in trouble?"

"No, I called the police. They said it's legal to hold a sign asking for money, but it becomes panhandling once you approach people or make direct contact."

"Are you sure?"

"That's what they said. I have the signs. You could work one side of the mall and I'll work the other. Come on, it will be fun."

The Sixteenth Street Mall was glowing with activity. The restaurants, bars and shops were brightly lit and crowded with people from every walk of life. There were musicians, police on horseback and even a team of street evangelists.

Upon arriving, we sat on the sidewalk near a busy corner. I handed Gloria one of the signs and said, "All you have to do is hold it up and smile. I'll be across the street."

"Don't leave me here!"

"Don't worry, I'll be back to check on you. Besides, you'll make more money without me hanging around."

As I watched Gloria from across the street, she appeared to be doing just fine. Every so often, someone would hand her a dollar or put change in her hand. People on my side only gave me dirty looks. I wasn't making any money, so after a while, I walked down the street to see what the evangelists were doing.

I could hear someone yelling about Jesus from the distance, and as I approached, I watched different members of their organization taking turns sharing testimonies, while others handed out Bible tracts. The evangelists were all wearing bright yellow T-shirts and were making such a commotion, everyone who passed by had some kind of reaction.

Many people stopped for a few minutes to listen before going on their way. Others from the crowd were engaged in conversation, and a few had their heads bowed towards the ground, as if they were praying.

I asked a young couple who stopped to listen if they believed in Jesus and shared parts of my testimony. They believed in a higher power and were interested in developing a personal relationship with God, but just as our conversation heated up, I felt an overwhelming need to get back and check on Gloria.

Over an hour had passed, and as I approached the corner where she was sitting, I realized two drunk men had taken up her cause. One was staggering back and forth on the sidewalk, demanding that people give her money. The other guy was sitting next to her saying things like, "Hey, baby. I'll get you a hotel room. Just you and me, baby, all night long."

"Where did you go?" she asked when she saw me coming.

"I'm sorry. I went to check out the missionaries. Come on, let's get out of here."

I took Gloria by the hand, and we ran across the street and jumped on the shuttle bus. We rode to the end of mall and sat down on a park bench underneath a streetlight.

"How much money did you get?" I asked.

She emptied several handfuls of change from her pocket and unfolded the bills. She only had $11.85.

"I have $6," I said. "But it's not enough. The cheapest hotel is going to be around $30."

As we discussed possible options, Gloria's countenance fell and my heart broke. It was a little after 10 p.m. I was tired, and Gloria had just been traumatized by more abusive men. I kept asking the Lord what He wanted me to do, but couldn't hear any answers. Finally, I made a decision.

"I don't know why the Lord called me to live on the streets, but I think it's more about serving people than sleeping in a shelter. If you want, we could ride the bus to my parents' house, pick up my truck and you could sleep at my house.

"I know this whole thing sounds weird. I don't take people in off the streets, but because you offered to share your hotel room, it's the least I can do for you. And let me reiterate, it's not a sexual thing. Nothing like that will happen."

"Are you sure you don't mind? I'll give you the money," she said.

"That's not necessary, you can keep it."

Upon arriving at my house, we were both hungry and thirsty, so I made chicken tacos for dinner. Soon the conversation turned towards the Christian walk. We spoke about going to church in the morning and made plans for the 9 a.m. service. I felt an overwhelming desire to help and continued digging deeper into her situation.

"How are you going to work things out with your boyfriend?" I asked.

"I don't know."

"If not, you'll need a place to stay tomorrow."

"I don't get paid till Friday."

"I'm sure we could find some rental assistance to help. Have you prayed about it?"

"Not really."

"As a Christian, I'm sure you know how to make your decisions in prayer. Jesus is not just Lord Sunday morning in church for an hour. He needs to be Lord over every aspect of your life and relationships — whom you date, live with and marry. Is the Lord calling you and your boyfriend into marriage?"

"I doubt it," she said.

"I used to go through the same thing years ago, and it caused me a lot of grief. I hit the bars to find tall, beautiful blondes with big hair. I would date them for a while and end up having sex a month later.

"I never had plans to marry these women, I just used them for good times and social recognition. Eventually our issues conflicted, we would start fighting, go through a painful breakup, and I would start the process all over again.

"Finally, I realized the Lord wasn't going to bring me the woman of my dreams until I put Him first. I made a vow of celibacy until marriage, because premarital sex is a sin called fornication. You do know that, right?"

"I know."

"After making my vow, I still went out on dates, but soon found it inappropriate to make romantic advances towards women because the fun had to stop somewhere. A kiss on the cheek seemed innocent enough, but a week later, we were making out and removing clothes.

"Now, I don't make any romantic advances towards women unless God is calling me down the road towards marriage. I pray for my future wife everyday. I'm open to meeting and being friends with everyone, but I'll never get trapped in another dead-end relationship.

"One day, God will bring me the woman of my dreams. We'll fall in love, get married and consummate the union afterwards."

"That sounds too good to be true."

"God wants his best for everyone. All you need to do is hear from Him on your current boyfriend situation. If God's calling you into marriage, you'll need to work out your issues and walk down the aisle. If not, you're facing a painful breakup and will need a new place to live. Either way it's going to be hard, but don't worry. God's faithful to those who trust in His ways."

"It all seems overwhelming right now," said Gloria.

"That's why you need to be in serious prayer."

After dinner I gathered some blankets and a pillow and placed them on the couch. "Good night," I said and headed upstairs to my room for the evening.

Twenty

The next morning, Gloria and I drove to Calvary Community Church, located high on a hill overlooking a small lake. As we pulled into the lower parking lot, the reflection of the bell tower on the water's edge caught my attention. The steeple-like structure was crowned with a gold cross, and its reflection extended halfway across the lake.

After joining a crowd of people hurrying towards the front door and taking our seats in the back row, I began praying. *Lord, please move on Gloria's heart. Forgive her sinfulness, heal her woundedness. Draw her into your loving arms. Fill her with your spirit and give her wisdom regarding her boyfriend.*

As I continued to pray, the pastor started preaching on God's love. His compelling message touched my heart, and when I looked over at Gloria, I noticed she had streams of tears rolling down her face.

"I have to go, I'm sorry. Where's the rest room?" She said.

It took her a long time to return, and after the service ended, she seemed emotionally distant, as if she were deep in thought. "What's going on?" I asked.

"I wonder if there's a pay phone. I probably should call."

"Let's go over to the grocery store on the corner."

After a ten-minute call to her boyfriend, Gloria came back with a look of relief on her face. "He's taking me back. Can you give me a ride to Alameda and Union?"

"Good job working things out with your boyfriend, but don't forget, the Lord loves you and has a plan for your life. He wants to protect you, but He's not going to violate your free will. If you ignore His warnings and keep putting yourself in compromising situations, He will allow you to suffer the natural consequences of your actions."

As we arrived at the corner of Alameda and Union, I handed Gloria a copy of my book and said, "Take care, I'll keep you in my prayers."

"Thanks for everything! I'll never forget how you helped me."

As I watched her walk away, I was flooded with an overwhelming spirit of joy. It felt like the Lord was rewarding me. The peaceful presence that filled my heart made all the hardships worthwhile. The weekend was over before I knew it, and I couldn't wait to call Cindy.

"Hey, I'm back."

"How come you didn't call sooner? What happened? I imagined you riding a bus all night trying to stay warm."

"I'm sorry. I ended up taking a woman home last night."

"The Lord calls you on a spiritual journey, and you end up taking a date home last night?"

"Very funny. It wasn't a date, it was ministry. The woman hadn't been in church for years, and she's stuck in an abusive relationship. It was dangerous for her to be out on the streets alone."

"You know I'm joking," Cindy said in her playful voice. "Tell me what happened."

"I learned a great deal of humility. I had so much pride, I could barely hold my sign in public. I had to surrender my desire to look good and need for approval before I could humble myself enough to beg.

"I also learned about dependence. I have been financially successful my entire life. Never have I depended on anyone, but when you're totally helpless, turning to the Lord takes on a whole new meaning.

"The biggest lesson was seeing God's relentless love for those in need. I spoke with a lot of hurting people. Their stories touched my heart. Just thinking how God provides for His children brings tears to my eyes."

"It sounds like your weekend was a huge success," Cindy said.

"If you say so. I'm just glad it's over. What was yours like?"

"I was out there dying to self with ya."

"What do you mean? I hear that phrase all the time, but never quite got it."

"I received a collect call from a distant friend who needed to borrow $500 for bond. He's going through a divorce and was arrested after leaving the bar late last night. A part of me wanted to help, but as I lay in bed, another part didn't want to get up.

"I was faced with a difficult decision. Should I put my flesh to death and act in love, or make selfish excuses? The two sides were in direct conflict. God wants me to love and serve my neighbors, my flesh wants to be comfortable, safe and secure.

"Finally, I made a decision for Christ. I put my needs and concerns aside for those of my friend. I got up in the middle of the night and bonded him out of jail. As I allowed a small part of myself to die last night, God filled my heart with peace and blessed my efforts."

"How come you call it 'dying to self?' And why didn't you wait till morning?"

"Because if I were in jail, I would want my friends to come immediately. Besides, according to John 12:24-25, dying to self is a required part of the Christian walk. *Very truly, I tell you, unless a grain of wheat falls into the earth and dies, it remains just a single grain; but if it dies, it bears much fruit. Those who love their life lose it, and those who hate their life in this world will keep it for eternal life.*

"Once a grain of wheat is buried underground it no longer lives for itself, but changes into a sprout. It surrenders its very existence for the opportunity to produce thirty, sixty, or ninety fold at harvest time. If it never dies, it never produces."

"Maybe your friend needed a night in jail to sober up," I said.

"It's not about teaching other people lessons. He's

already in enough pain. I'm the one who needs to put my selfishness aside to produce more fruit for the kingdom of God."

"I see what you're saying. I had to put my selfishness to death before I could spend the weekend helping Gloria."

"Exactly, but don't think the process of dying to self happens in a day. It's a lifelong journey. Just look at the life of Jesus. He put the will of the Father first and foremost. It didn't matter if He felt like getting whipped, kicked or spit upon. He put His fleshly concerns aside and walked in obedience, even to the point of death.

"And check out the quote from my devotionals this morning. It's from Galatians 6:7-8, *Do not be deceived; God is not mocked, for you reap whatever you sow. If you sow to your own flesh, you will reap corruption from the flesh; but if you sow to the Spirit, you will reap eternal life from the Spirit.*"

"I'm glad you shared that, Cindy. It gives me something to think about. Thanks again, we'll talk soon."

Twenty-One

$\mathcal{A}$ week later, I found myself stopped at a busy downtown intersection. Turning to look out my window, I noticed a homeless man wearing a dirty red ski jacket, faded blue jeans and black boots. He was walking back and forth on the sidewalk holding a sign that said, Homeless, please help, God bless. As he approached my car, I looked away, because I didn't feel like giving him any money.

Soon after the light turned green the Lord starting convicting me. I felt terrible for diverting my eyes from a man in need, especially because I knew exactly what it felt like. *But Lord, I don't want to go back. The guy's a drunk who just wants money to support his habit.*

The further I drove from the intersection, the more internal anguish my conscience produced. Eventually, I couldn't take it anymore, and I cried out, "You win. I'm sorry. I'm turning around and going back. See? I'm going to help, just don't withhold your sweet intimacy from me."

After parking my vehicle at a nearby restaurant, I walked up to the corner where the man was standing. Not knowing what to say, I pretended to be crossing the street. Finally, I summoned enough courage and said, "Hey man, do you got the time?"

Taking a watch with a broken band from his pocket he said, "4:45."

"Your sign says you're in need of help. What can I do for you?"

"Can you spare a few bucks?"

"I don't think money's your problem. I could give you a thousand dollars, and a month later you would still be holding that sign."

"What do you know? I have nothing."

"Why don't you get a job?"

"I'm homeless! I can't get cleaned up, I haven't bathed in months. These are the only clothes I own. You have no idea what it's like out here."

"Actually, I do, and for $20 we could go to the thrift store and get you a whole new wardrobe — new pants, a clean shirt, a different jacket. You'll look great for an interview."

"I can't get a job, I don't have an address. What am I supposed to say, *sleeping in bushes near Platte River?*"

"You can use my P.O. box and cell number. If someone calls, what's your name?"

"Jim."

"If someone calls for Jim, I'll take the information and set an interview a day later. Just call and check messages on a regular basis. Once you get a job, I'll help you find a place to live."

"It will never work."

"Sure it will. A cheap hotel's only $30 a day, times a week, that's $210. We could get new clothes at a thrift store, a bag of food, and I'll drive you around to construction sites for a labor job. If you worked a forty-hour week at $10 an hour, you could pay rent and still have some left over.

"But like I said, your problem's not money, it's drinking."

"Yeah, I drink, so what?"

"How much?"

"A half-gallon of vodka a day."

"It's a problem because no one wants to hire a drunk. If you can't be responsible and go to work, you're not going to make any money. No money, no place to stay. Like I said, I could snap my fingers and have you off the streets in a second. But first, you'll have to stop drinking."

"I'm not going to quit. I had jobs before and after a hard day's work, I need a beer."

"Have it your way," I said, turning to leave.

"Hey, where you going?"

"I'm out of here."

"Can you spare a few bucks?"

"To support your drinking habit — no way! I offered you a new life. All you have to do is stop pouring poison into your body. If you're not serious about helping yourself, then I want nothing to do with you."

"I'm serious. I hate it out here. I want to work, I just need help."

After feeling a deep sense of compassion stirring in my heart, I said, "Meet me here tomorrow morning at nine. I'm curious to see if you'll show up. If you do, I'll take you shopping at the thrift store."

"I'll be here. This corner, right? 9 a.m.?"

"See you tomorrow," I said, running back across the street.

Later that evening, I had dinner plans with Cindy at a quaint French restaurant located near Main Street in Golden. The restaurant came highly recommended by one of her friends. The owners had converted an old Victorian home into an elegant dining experience.

As I approached the two-story building, I noticed Cindy gliding back and forth on a porch swing. Her black jacket and long blonde hair blowing in the breeze made a striking image against the old-fashioned decor, which was illuminated by floodlights.

"Don't you just love this place?" I asked, taking a seat on a bench across from her.

"And the latticework. I'll bet it took forever to paint the trim all the different shades of purple, mauve and pink," she said.

Within a few minutes our names were called and the host led us upstairs to a quiet table in front of a bay window. We ordered bouillabaisse to start, a bottle of Beaujolais and duck aux poivre for the main course.

After describing my latest homeless adventure, Cindy leaned back in her chair and said, "The Lord keeps giving me a message to share with you. I have been hesitant till now, but maybe tonight's your night."

"I'm listening."

"It has to do with your ability to love from the heart. You have great internal depth and are very generous, but you never allow anyone inside."

"What are you talking about?"

"It's not about romantic attraction. You're one of my closest and dearest friends but we never connect on a deep, heartfelt level. I have tried many times, but it's like you have protective walls that keep me out."

"You're right, I don't make myself vulnerable, because people always latch onto me with their pain and problems."

"Am I one of those who burden you with problems?"

"No, I care deeply for you. Your friendship means the world to me."

"Do you love me?"

"I don't know. What do you mean — love?"

"Because I love you." Cindy said, as tears began welling up in her eyes.

After a long period of silence, she continued. "Love is a function of the heart. If you never remove the guard walls and allow people inside, then you can never truly love. Please don't misunderstand me. I'm not talking about a romantic, dating love known as Eros, but the spiritual love, agape.

"Jesus loved everyone from the heart. That's why huge crowds were drawn to Him. He connected with people on a deep, intimate level. He didn't walk around with protective boundaries. He wasn't scared of vulnerability, getting hurt or embracing other people's pain. Unconditional love and compassion flowed from His heart like a mighty river."

Taking a small Bible from her purse, Cindy read a quote from 1 John 4:7, 8, 20, 21. *Beloved, let us love one another, because love is from God; everyone who loves is born of God and knows God. Whoever does not love does not know God, for God is love. Those who say, 'I love God,' and hate their brothers or sisters, are liars; for those who do not love a brother or sister whom they have seen, cannot love God whom they have not seen. The commandment we have from him is this: those who love God must love their brothers and sisters also.*

"God wants to bring His love into the world through your heart. I was there on the mountaintop when you invited Christ inside. He honored your request, and now you have a deep wellspring to share with your brothers and sisters. I believe God is calling you to remove your walls and allow His beauty to shine forth into the world."

"I don't want to share. The world is full of lowlife heathens, who will trample my precious heart."

"Jesus loved everyone and as a follower, you're required to do the same. That's what the Christian walk is all about. Once you remove the guarded walls, those, quote *'heathens'* will see something different in you and will want to acquire it themselves."

"I hear what you're saying, but I'm already doing ministry. In fact, I'm taking a stinky bum out tomorrow to buy clothes."

"First of all, God's love is not yours to withhold.

And what makes you any different than a homeless man in God's eyes? Except for your noisy gong. A life devoid of love is empty and lonely. How do you expect to fall in love with your future wife when you can't share a small part of your heart with your friends?"

"I don't know how to remove the walls," I said. "They've been there my entire life."

"Young children are not born with guarded hearts. They are open, loving and trusting, until they get hurt. Usually an abusive parent or unhealthy boyfriend/girlfriend comes along and impedes our ability."

"I'm sick of healing work. I have done everything I know."

"Maybe this kind of work you can't do on your own. Surrender the situation over to the Lord. Ask Him to break your heart of stone and give you a heart of love alone."

Twenty-Two

As I drove downtown to meet Jim the following day, I continued thinking about the words Cindy had spoken. The Holy Spirit also confirmed the same reality within me. I did have huge walls. Not only did they keep me distant from my friend's love, but they also prevented me from giving and receiving God's love.

Instead of protecting my heart, I wanted to open up a huge pipeline, to tap into the endless supply of God's love and allow it to flow through me, into the lives of others.

As I pondered how that would work, I parked my truck near the corner of 6th and Speer. To my surprise, Jim was standing where he had promised. "Good morning," I said. "I didn't think you'd show up."

"I was thinking the same thing about you."

"Maybe this is our first lesson in trusting one another. Are you ready?"

"For what?"

"Shopping. We'll grab some clothes at a thrift store, stop by Supercuts for a trim, and within a few hours, you'll be a new man."

"I ain't got no money."

"Don't worry. Instead of tithing to my church this week, I'm going to spend it on you."

As we drove to the thrift store, the smell just about killed me. I had the windows rolled down and still couldn't breathe. Jim wasn't joking. He hadn't bathed in months.

He would panhandle enough money to buy a bottle and then pass out drunk every night. Every so often he pitched in money with other street dwellers to rent a motel room for the night. It was an ongoing cycle of destruction that he couldn't seem to rise above.

At the thrift store, we picked out a pair of black jeans, two long-sleeve shirts and a gray sports coat, all for $13. There wasn't any place for Jim to change, so we walked across the street to a convenience store to use their rest room. Once there, Jim wanted to shave, so I loaned him two more dollars for a razor.

He was in the bathroom a long time and when he finally came out, I was amazed. He looked great. Jim was a handsome, thirty-year-old man with a great tan from being outside in the sun all day. His long blonde hair was pulled back in a ponytail, and the jacket with combat boots made him look rugged, yet sophisticated. He didn't want a haircut, so after filling him full of compliments, I dropped him back at his intersection.

"Here's my cell number and P.O. box. Why don't you spend the rest of the day looking for work?"

"I used to work at a gas station. They're always looking for help," Jim said as he waved good-bye.

"Call and check messages, I'm sure you'll have a job soon."

Several days passed without any news from Jim, so I drove past his intersection to see what was happening. There he was, wearing his red ski jacket and holding the same old sign.

It made me furious. Grabbing my Bible, I walked over to set him straight. "Hey Jim, how come you're not out looking for work?"

"I was wondering what happened to you. Did I get any phone calls? I filled out two applications. The sport coat's in my bag over there. I didn't want it getting dirty."

"Sorry, no calls. Job hunting is going to require more effort than two applications. You have to follow up. If the company doesn't have an immediate position available, your application could sit in a file for months. But like I said, drinking is going to be a major problem. You need to quit. No one is going to hire a drunk."

"I need my drinks, or else I have seizures. I have watched guys die because they couldn't get a drink in time. I already get the shakes real bad. I can't quit!"

"Did you know drunkenness is a major sin? Deuteronomy 21:18-21 says: *If someone has a stubborn and rebellious son who will not obey his father and mother, who does not heed them when they discipline him, then his father and his mother shall take hold of him and bring him out to the elders of his town at the gate of that place. They shall say to the elders of his town, 'This son of ours is stubborn and rebellious. He will not obey us. He is a glutton and a drunkard.' Then all the men of the town shall stone him to death. So you shall purge the evil from your midst; and all Israel will hear, and be afraid.*

"I'm sure glad you're not living back in Old

Testament times, because stubborn, rebellious drunkards were stoned to death. No mercy. An angry mob
would have pelted you with rocks until your bloody
corpse stopped breathing."

"I know the Bible, too," Jim said.

"Good, do you know Galatians 5:19-21? Drunkards
will not inherit the kingdom of Heaven: *Now the works of
the flesh are obvious: fornication, impurity, licentiousness, idolatry,
sorcery, enmities, strife, jealousy, anger, quarrels, dissensions, factions, envy, drunkenness, carousing, and things like these. I am
warning you, as I warned you before: those who do such things will
not inherit the kingdom of God."*

"If that's the kind of God you serve, I want nothing
to do with you," Jim said. "I don't know what kind of
weird religion you're from, but God loves me. *Nothing
can separate me from God's love.* That's what they say
every night at the Jesus shelter."

"Except sin. And you're right, God does love you. It
breaks His heart to see you suffer out here. God wants
to set you free from the bondage of Satan and alcoholism. Instead of justifying your behaviors with God's
love, why don't you take a serious look at your love for
God and do something with your life?"

Folding his sign in thirds, Jim grabbed his bag and
cut through the grass towards the bike trail. "Leave me
alone!" he screamed, as he disappeared behind the trees
alongside the Platte River.

"Good riddance, ya stinky drunkard," I muttered
under my breath, as I headed towards my truck.

Later that afternoon, I felt terrible. It seemed like the

Lord was mad at me for the way I treated Jim. The peaceful presence that filled my heart and accompanied me wherever I went was gone. Not knowing what to do, I called Cindy for help.

After I explained how Jim had stomped off, she said, "Good job. It sounds like you're helping the homeless more than the rest of us. And I agree with you that drinking is a problem, but preaching hell and brimstone is not going to help Jim's situation.

"Christian ministry is about sharing Christ's love with the world. Instead of focusing on Jim's sin, try connecting with his heart. Allow yourself to feel compassion for his situation."

"How's that going to help?"

"Because with sin comes the natural consequences of hurt and pain. Instead of focusing on Jim's sin, try focusing your love on the pain his sin is causing. When you touch Jim's hurt with God's love, his eyes will be opened and he will want to change on his own."

"How do I do that?"

"Love is a function of the heart. You'll need to lower your walls and allow Jim inside. Embrace his pain and connect with him on a genuine and heartfelt level. I know it's scary at first, but you can do it.

"I remember the first time I opened my heart in ministry. I was volunteering at a handicapped retreat center when I noticed a woman in a wheelchair. She was all alone in the corner. I wanted to reach out, but I felt uncomfortable having arms and legs when so many were without.

"Eventually, I walked over to see how she was doing, and we started to talk. Her name, Julie Pierson, sounded very familiar. After getting to know her, I realized she was the same woman my entire church had prayed for years prior.

"We never met, but during my prayer time, I pictured a beautiful young woman who had just moved here from Texas. She was picking up her son from school when a lumber truck collided with her sports car. Her little boy died in the accident, and she was paralyzed from the chest down.

"Upon meeting her, I noticed her health had taken a turn for the worse. She had lost a lot of weight and looked weakened by sickness. Instead of focusing on her physical condition, I looked past the wheelchair and into her heart. I viewed her as the same beautiful young woman from Texas and opened my heart to her in love.

"I can't explain how it works," Cindy continued, "but somehow God's love flowed through me and I was able to experience a deep sense of caring and compassion. A bond formed between us, which developed into a beautiful relationship.

"Afterwards, I understood the difference between the behaviors of ministry and allowing God's love to flow through my heart. That weekend, I had volunteered to serve others, but until I opened my heart, I was just going through the motions of ministry."

"I see what you're saying. When I took Jim to the thrift store, I didn't truly connect with him. I only helped out of obligation, because God wanted me to."

"You're doing a great job. Ministry has to start somewhere," Cindy said. "Keep seeking God in prayer. I'm sure He who began the good work in you will bring it to completion."

"Any suggestions?"

"Have you considered another Holy Week?"

"You mean ask God to break me after fasting all week? Now there's a brilliant idea. It's been good talking with ya, Cindy."

Twenty-Three

After a lot of prayer and consideration, I decided to embark on another Holy Week. If Cindy could fast for ten days on juice and water, surely I could endure seven. Besides, God always honored my efforts. Every time I requested to be more holy, God always fulfilled my heart's desire with His miracle-working power.

I began the week in prayer: *Lord, I dedicate the week to you. Please break me. Completely remove any ungodly hindrances from my life. Destroy the guarded walls that surround my heart. Help me to be a man of great love. Help me see your people with eyes of compassion and love them with the heart of Christ.*

The first few days of the fast were the hardest. I found myself getting physically tired in the afternoons. My body slowed down, but my spirit marched on in high gear. I was locked in a constant state of prayer and praise. I converted all my food hunger into God hunger and through His great love, He fed me supernaturally.

The morning of the third day, I looked up the word *love* in my concordance. There were hundreds of listings, so I began studying the biblical context of each quote to gain a deeper understanding. I started with 1 Corinthians 13:1-8:

If I speak in the tongues of mortals and of angels, but do not have love, I am a noisy gong or a clanging cymbal. And if I have prophetic powers, and understand all mysteries and all knowledge, and if I have all faith, so as to remove mountains, but do not have love, I am nothing. If I give away all my possessions, and if I hand over my body so that I may boast, but do not have love, I gain nothing. Love is patient; love is kind; love is not envious or boastful or arrogant or rude. It does not insist on its own way; it is not irritable or resentful; it does not rejoice in wrongdoing, but rejoices in the truth. It bears all things, believes all things, hopes all things, endures all things. Love never ends...

I wanted this same kind of love to flow through my heart like Cindy had described. I cared deeply for many people, but I wasn't in love with anyone. After taking a close look at all my relationships, I decided to start with my father.

During my childhood, my father and I had never been very close. After I moved out of his house, we made a commitment to say the words *I love you* every time we saw each other. We have continued the practice for years, but after saying the words over and over, I realized, I was unable to truly love him, because I never allowed him into my heart.

Later that evening, after a lot of prayer, I decided to create a deeper heartfelt relationship with him. I went over to my parents' house to somehow capture the essence of who my father was and accept him into my heart.

"Hi, Dad," I said, after walking through the front door. "What's going on?"

"Just finishing up with dinner and making my lunch for tomorrow."

I tried to carry on a conversation with him, but he was watching a television show in between banging pots and pans around. I felt like smashing the television and screaming, *Why can't you pay attention to me for just one minute?*

I wanted to change him. There were a lot of things about him I didn't like, but he was my father and I was there to love him unconditionally.

I began watching the television show with him and started to accept my father for who he was. I felt love entering my heart when I realized that all of the positive qualities I deeply valued in myself all existed and originated in him first.

"Thank you, Dad," I said.

"For what?"

"For being a good father to me. You're dependable, loyal, conservative, God-fearing, tall, handsome, health-conscious, hardworking and you know how to fix things with tools."

Immediately my father stopped what he was doing and sat down. He looked like he was going to cry. He didn't have much to say, but when I left that evening I could feel love in my heart. It was small at first, but enough to make me want to go back for more.

The next morning, on the fourth day of the fast, I arose early and headed over to St. Patrick's Church for a day of prayer. I brought along a large container of grapefruit juice and planned to spend the entire day practicing contemplative prayer.

I was having a hard time quieting my mind, because

unpleasant memories of my ex-fiancée kept interfering with my thoughts. I had given her my heart, and after I had suffered years of emotional abuse, we broke up. I was devastated and couldn't leave my house for months. It hurt so bad, I swore in my anger *to never love again.*

It didn't take long for God to bring the vow the enemy was using to my attention. I was able to renounce it in the name of Jesus and could feel the Lord setting me free. All I could do was lie there and cry. I released all my hurt and allowed God's love to penetrate the depths of my soul.

Several hours later, I continued the practice of contemplative prayer, and my thoughts began drifting off again. I tried to refocus my attention by creating a mental picture of Jesus. I was looking into His beautiful eyes, when suddenly, the vision took on a life of its own.

Jesus came to life in my imagination and abruptly turned His face from me. His facial expressions became hard and rigid. He was about to walk away, when I cried out, "Oh Lord, stop, please don't go!"

Immediately, I jumped up and started pacing back and forth. *What if Jesus really did turn His back on me?* The thought terrified me, because if He did, my life wouldn't be worth two cents. Could that happen? Every time I have sought the Lord in prayer, He's always been there.

Then it hit me like a ton of bricks. Jesus would never turn His back on me. But that's exactly what I had been doing to other people my entire life.

Quickly, I got back in prayer and made a promise to never again divert my eyes from another in need. His peaceful presence came rushing back when I realized the lesson He was teaching me. The Lord wanted me to love and connect with everyone, including Jim.

After leaving the church that afternoon, I drove downtown and parked my truck near the corner of 6th and Speer. As I approached the intersection, I noticed Jim leaning against a lightpost with his head bowed towards the ground.

"How's it going?" I asked.

"Monday's my worst day. It's like no one has any money after the weekend."

"I need to apologize for Bible thumping you the other day. It grieves my heart to see you suffer out here. I just wanted to help, but after thinking about it, maybe you enjoy life on the streets. You appear quite comfortable, no responsibilities, getting everything for free. It must be fun."

"I hate being homeless! It sucks out here!"

"Tell me what it's like."

"Every week cops harass me. They pour my drinks out and tell me to leave town. I have been hit by cars. Once a woman tried to kill me. My shopping cart got stuck in her bumper. She drug it halfway down the street and didn't even stop. I could die out here, and no one would care."

"I care, and I'm sorry. You don't deserve to be treated like that. You have tremendous value and unlimited potential. You're better than this. Don't let people treat you like that. Take control of your life. If you could do anything, what would it be? What do you live for?"

"I don't know. Beer, I guess."

"Besides beer. Do you have goals? Did you have any childhood dreams, like being an astronaut or flying airplanes?"

"No. My father told me I would never amount to anything. He beat my mom. I hate my father for leaving and my stepfather for what he did."

"Before we go any further, let's break that curse your father put on you. *You will amount to something!* God loves you and has big plans for your life. Don't let your father's words of condemnation and abuse stop you. If you feel like praying, we can renounce those words."

"Sure," Jim said, removing his hat and bowing his head towards the ground.

"Father God, we break all curses in the name of Jesus and send them back with your blessing. We ask you to turn Jim's life upside down and help him get off the streets."

"Amen," Jim said.

"If you want, I'll come back tomorrow and you can finish telling me about your father."

"You know where to find me," Jim said, as I turned to leave.

On the seventh day of the fast, I went over to St. Patrick's Church for more prayer. Around noon I ran out of juice, so I drove to the local supermarket to get more. I wanted to walk up and down the aisles to look at all the food, but I felt totally vulnerable and exposed. For some reason, people were intentionally staring at me.

Immediately, I checked the way I was dressed. My fly was zipped, my shirt was tucked in and I wasn't dragging anything around by my shoe. I didn't know what was wrong, but it felt like people could see right through me.

It was so uncomfortable, I grabbed the first bottle of orange juice I came across and proceeded towards the checkout line where a man confronted me. By the way he was looking, it felt like he was challenging me to a fight. I made eye contact briefly and then turned away. I couldn't wait to get back to church where it was safe.

Later that evening, I had plans to meet Cindy at the Soup & Salad Company near her house. After enduring an incredibly intense week of spiritual work, my first choice of places to break the fast was a five-star restaurant, but she suggested I'd be better off with something light to start.

Upon arriving, I loaded every item the salad bar had to offer on my plate. After smothering everything in creamy ranch dressing and croutons, I grabbed several pieces of cornbread and headed towards a table in the back. I was so hungry, I cleaned my entire plate and within minutes started feeling sick. I had an awful headache and could feel myself growing more irritable by the minute.

"I'm excited to hear about your Holy Week," Cindy said in her cheerful voice. "I have been praying for you every day."

"God did something terrible to me at the supermarket."

"What happened?"

"I went to buy juice and it felt like I was walking around in my underwear. Before, I wore a heavy trench coat of protection that no one could penetrate. Somehow God removed my protective walls, and now it seems like everyone can see right through me."

"That's wonderful!"

"No, it's not. I hate feeling this way!"

"Why, what's wrong?"

"People were staring at me. I think they could sense the presence of Christ. Towards the end of the fast, I was living off the power of God. His anointing was so strong, I must have been glowing. Without my guarded walls, I feel vulnerable and exposed."

"Don't worry. God's not going to do anything that's not in your best interest. I know it makes you uncomfortable, but I think it's beautiful," Cindy said, taking a small Bible from her purse.

"Let me read Luke 8:16-18: *No one after lighting a lamp hides it under a jar, or puts it under a bed, but puts it on a lampstand, so that those who enter may see the light. For nothing is hidden that will not be disclosed, nor is anything secret that will not become known and come to light. Then pay attention to how you listen; for to those who have, more will be given; and from those who do not have, even what they seem to have will be taken away.*

"Because you have been given much, much will be required. Your heart is like a crystal lamp, and you're required to let the light of Christ shine forth in a world of darkness. You have done a tremendous job removing the darkness of sin and emotional baggage from your life. Now it's time to remove the walls and allow your inner beauty to shine forth for all to see. Don't be afraid, it's a beautiful work God is doing."

Twenty-Four

$\mathcal{I}$t took me several months to accept the fact that I no longer had protective walls. It felt like everyone could sense my emotions from across the room. Happy or sad, I could no longer hide anything.

The gift of openness worked best with the homeless population along the Platte River. Street people didn't trust anyone and without my protective walls, they could see my true agenda. I had no ulterior motives, other than genuine compassion and a burning desire to serve God.

My ability to be open with Jim also helped him trust me with his deepest childhood wounds. I realized this one rainy afternoon when the topic of his father's abuse came up again. We were taking cover underneath a bridge, when I asked, "Has your father ever done anything nice?"

"I hate my father. After the last fight, he broke my mother's arm and never came back."

"I know, but was there ever a time when he wasn't drinking?"

"Once he took me to the stadium and bought me a Red Sox pennant. I carried it around forever. Then it got lost."

"If your father's abusive when he's drunk and nice when he's sober, then your anger should be focused on the evil of alcoholism and not towards him personally. I'm sure your father loved you the best he could. He probably grew up with an abusive, alcoholic father himself."

"How did you know about my grandfather?"

"Because the sins of the father are passed down to the third and fourth generation. Didn't you say you had two kids in Alabama?"

"Yeah. Theresa and Alex."

"Do you love them?"

"Yeah, I do."

"You're mad at your father for abandoning you, and yet you did the same thing to poor little Theresa and Alex."

"She made me. It's not my fault. My ex-wife got a restraining order!"

"Instead of talking about how alcoholism is directly responsible for the restraining order, let's look at the situation from your kids' point of view.

"Two beautiful young children who need their father's love, but you're out here getting drunk. In the same way, you needed your father's love when he was out getting drunk. I know you're doing the best you can and love your children, just as your father loved you and did the best he could."

Upon hearing these words, Jim's cold, hard exterior melted into the demeanor of a hurt little boy. For the first time ever, I saw his eyes fill with tears, and he curled up into a ball as if he was experiencing severe cramps.

Moving closer to put my arm around him, I said, "You don't have to die out here. I spoke with detox. They'll give you Transzeen for your withdrawals. They check blood pressure every two hours to prevent seizures. It will be like a minivacation. Afterwards, I'll help you get a job with people who like you and a place to live."

"I'm scared," Jim said.

"I'll stand with you. There's nothing to fear."

Staggering over to the bushes where he stashed his bottle of vodka, Jim removed the cap and hurled the bottle into the Platte River. "I'm ready for a new life!" he shouted.

Upon arriving at the detox facility, Jim looked at me with worry in his eyes and said, "Are you sure?"

"Let's pray," I said, taking his hand. "Heavenly Father, please give Jim the strength he needs for recovery. We take authority over the spirit of alcoholism. We bind all demonic forces and cast them into the abyss to never again return. Come Holy Spirit, fill Jim with your wisdom, love and fortitude. Give him the strength to stand victorious in Jesus' name."

Once inside the facility, we were greeted by a lady in a white nurse's uniform, who began the intake procedure. She asked Jim a series of questions about his history and had him blow into a Breathalyzer.

As we waited for the results, I found myself getting curious and started walking around. There were many rows of military-style cots covered with white sheets and pillows. Most of the clients were in a room watching television. Some were lying down, and a few were talking on the pay phones in the cafeteria.

When I came back, the nurse was helping Jim remove his boots.

"How long will you hold him?" I asked.

"By law, until he blows zeros. If he's sick or running a high blood pressure, up to four or five days. It all depends on how hard he comes down."

Putting my hand on Jim's shoulder I said, "It sounds like you're in good hands. I'll be back to visit you tomorrow."

Five days later, they released Jim. I went to pick him up and found him sitting outside smoking cigarette butts other people had left in the ashtray.

"What are you doing?"

"Snippes are good for ya. Can't give everything up at once," he said, taking another drag.

"Are you strong enough to start work?"

"I'm still a little shaky, but feeling much better."

"I called a framing contractor I knew back when I was building townhomes. He's always looking for labor and pays $9 to start. I told him you're a hard worker with tool bags, but in need of a ride every day. He lives close to Broadway and Hampden and is willing to pick you up tomorrow morning at 6:30."

"I don't know about construction, and where am I going to get tools?"

"Construction's easy. Anyone can hump lumber. We'll stop by a pawnshop and, for $30, get everything you'll need."

"Where am I going to stay tonight?"

"I was going to rent you a motel room for a week, but after calling around, I found the Working Man's Depot. It's like a shelter, except you buy a bed for $35 a week. You're required to have a full-time job, and they even have an Antabuse program."

"I can't take Antabuse, it's bad for my liver."

"Like alcohol's good for your liver? Besides, it's not like you have a lot of options. I'll pay your first week's rent and loan you money for the tools."

"Shelters remind me of the army barracks."

"Let's go check it out. If you don't like it, we'll find something else."

After acquiring everything Jim needed to start his new life, I was exhausted. It was hard enough getting him sober and employed. Now Jim needed solid Christian friends. He needed a new way of coping with life's problems. He needed to hang around a guy like Scott.

We hadn't spoken in a while, so I gave Scott a call and said, "Hey brother, I was wondering if you would take a friend of mine to church Sunday."

"Sure, I would be happy to. What's up?"

"I have been working with a homeless man named Jim. He doesn't have any friends and needs male discipleship."

"You're joking, right? I can't take a bum to church."

"He's not homeless anymore. He's staying at the Working Man's Depot. He's clean, sober, employed, stable and on Antabuse. All you have to do is pick him up downtown and maybe take him out to lunch."

"It's not going to work," Scott said.

"Why not? I thought it was a biblical requirement for all Christians to love and serve those in need. John 13:34-35 says, *I give you a new commandment, that you love one another. Just as I have loved you, you also should love one another. By this everyone will know that you are my disciples, if you have love for one another.*"

"I'm already a disciple. The Bible says I'm saved by faith apart from works."

"I'm not calling to get into another theological argument. Jim's finally in a stable environment, but he won't last long without help from other believers. I worked really hard and don't want to see him fall back into his old ways."

"That's exactly why the Bible says, 'Your righteous deeds are like filthy rags.' You can work with the guy for months, but unless he comes to the saving knowledge of Jesus Christ he's going to fall down every time. Without Jesus, there's nothing you can do."

"Trust me. No one gets a man into detox without the Lord's help. I have been interceding on Jim's behalf for months. And where do you get off with the filthy rags quote? I can't believe the Bible would say such a thing."

"Isaiah 64:6."

"On second thought, don't worry about taking Jim to church. I'll do it myself."

Twenty-Five

*A*fter getting off the phone with Scott, I went straight for my NIV to read the verse he had quoted.

You come to the help of those who gladly do right, who remember your ways. But when we continued to sin against them, you were angry. How then can we be saved? All of us have become like one who is unclean, and all our righteous acts are like filthy rags; we all shrivel up like a leaf, and like the wind our sins sweep us away. No one calls on your name or strives to lay hold of you; for you have hidden your face from us and made us waste away because of our sins. Yet, O Lord, you are our Father. We are the clay, you are the potter; we are all the work of your hand. Do not be angry beyond measure, O Lord; do not remember our sins forever. Oh, look upon us, we pray, for we are all your people.

After reading Isaiah 64:5-9 over and over again in prayer, I studied the previous and prior chapters to gain a better understanding of what the author (Isaiah) was saying to his audience. Once I understood God's message to the people of that time, I was able to apply the information to my own life.

"Hey Scott. I'm calling you back on the filthy rags quote."

"I'm listening."

"In the larger context, Isaiah and God are speaking back and forth in conversation. When the Israelites distance themselves from God, they fell into enemy hands. After turning back, God rescued them time and time again. It's a recurring theme in the Old Testament.

"In chapter 64, the prophet Isaiah is offering a prayer of repentance on Israel's behalf. Just like if I said, *Forgive the modern day church, Lord, we're all a bunch of complacent sinners and no one calls on your name.*

"That doesn't mean everyone in today's church is living in sin or has stopped praying. The passage only reflects the spiritual depravity of the people. It's not a direct teaching on works or the requirement of works for the salvation process."

"I don't have time for this," Scott said. Ephesians 2:8-9 says: *For by grace you have been saved through faith, and this is not your own doing; it is the gift of God — not the result of works, so that no one may boast."*

"Keep reading, Scott. You left out the last line of that verse," I said. "Ephesians 2:10 continues on to say, *For we are what he has made us, created in Christ Jesus for good works, which God prepared beforehand to be our way of life.*

"I agree with the entire quote, taken in context. We are saved by *grace* alone! No one deserves to go to Heaven. It's a tremendous gift from God. We are saved by grace alone, but not by faith alone. No one works their way to Heaven, but don't think for a second that works are not a required part of the salvation process, because James 2:14-17, 26 says they are.

What good is it, my brothers and sisters, if you say you have faith but do not have works? Can faith save you? If a brother or sis-

ter is naked and lacks daily food, and one of you says to them, "Go in peace; keep warm and eat your fill," and yet you do not supply their bodily needs, what is the good of that? So faith by itself, if it has no works, is dead. For just as the body without the spirit is dead, so faith without works is also dead.

"The Bible never says faith is the only requirement for the salvation process. Faith without works is dead. Hence, I'm saved by a faith which produces good works."

"I'm saved by faith alone," Scott argued back defensively.

"Let's take one quote at a time. We started out with filthy rags from Isaiah. Clearly the verse has nothing to do with the salvation process. Therefore, you shouldn't be using it in that context. Let's pray over Isaiah and allow God to open our minds to its meaning, before we go any further."

"I'm not interested in praying over a verse. The entire Bible flows together as a whole. The only requirement for salvation is faith, and it has nothing to do with works. Romans 3:28 makes that point clear. *For we hold that a person is justified by faith apart from works prescribed by the law.* Maybe you need to educate yourself on Romans before we continue this conversation further!"

"You're right, I'll study Romans 3:28 and get back to you. Here's my problem. Are you open to hear me?"

"Sure, go ahead," Scott said.

"The authoritative word of God, the Bible, is not going to contradict itself. I see you taking a few lines of Romans and Ephesians and building another gospel that directly conflicts with the words of Jesus. That's why I wanted to pray over these passages and allow God's spirit to confirm the truth."

"What do you mean, Romans conflicts with the teachings of Jesus?"

"The book doesn't conflict, it's your interpretation. You just finished telling me how works have nothing to do with the salvation process. But in the twenty-fifth chapter of Matthew, the Lord says it does.

"Jesus gives three different parables. In the first, He compares the Christian walk to bridesmaids, five wise and five foolish. They were all part of the wedding party and were all guests of honor at the banquet, but the foolish were not allowed inside. Why?

"Because they failed to perform the necessary works to keep their lamps burning bright. In the same way, we're called to do the necessary works to keep our lights shining brightly in a world of darkness.

"In the second parable, Jesus compares the Christian walk to servants who have been given responsibilities and entrusted with talents. The good servants do their work and produced for the master's kingdom. The bad servants who fail to produce are thrown into the outer darkness where there will be weeping and gnashing of teeth.

"The third parable is the best of all, because Jesus is specifically talking about Judgment Day. He says all nations will be gathered before Him to give an account of their works. All nations meaning everyone. All Jews, all Gentiles and all Christians. Those who have per-formed good works enter into eternal life and those without, eternal separation. Matthew 25:31-46 reads:

When the Son of Man comes in his glory, and all the angels with him, then he will sit on the throne of his glory. All the nations will be gathered before him, and he will separate people one from another as a shepherd separates the sheep from the goats, and he will put the sheep at his right hand and the goats at the left. Then the king will say to those at his right hand, 'Come, you that are blessed by my Father, inherit the kingdom prepared for you from the foundation of the world; for I was hungry and you gave me food, I was thirsty and you gave me something to drink, I was a stranger and you welcomed me, I was naked and you gave me clothing, I was sick and you took care of me, I was in prison and you visited me.'

Then the righteous will answer him, 'Lord, when was it that we saw you hungry and gave you food, or thirsty and gave you something to drink? And when was it that we saw you a stranger and welcomed you, or naked and gave you clothing? And when was it that we saw you sick or in prison and visited you?' And the king will answer them, 'Truly I tell you, just as you did it to one of the least of these who are members of my family, you did it to me.'

Then he will say to those at his left hand, 'You that are accursed, depart from me into the eternal fire prepared for the devil and his angels; for I was hungry and you gave me no food, I was thirsty and you gave me nothing to drink, I was a stranger and you did not welcome me, naked and you did not give me clothing, sick and in prison and you did not visit me.' Then they also will answer, 'Lord, when was it that we saw you hungry or thirsty or a stranger or naked or sick or in prison, and did not take care of you?' Then he will answer them, 'Truly I tell you, just as you did not do it to one of the least of these, you did not do it to me.' And these will go away into eternal punishment, but the righteous into eternal life."

"Those parables can be interpreted many different ways," Scott said.

"That's why I wanted to pray. Why don't you ask God to open your mind and heart to Matthew 25 and Isaiah 64, and I'll do the same with Romans."

"Sounds good," Scott said, "we'll talk soon."

Twenty-Six

Almost a week went by without a call from Scott, so I decided to drop by his house for a visit. Upon my arrival, I saw his green Jeep Cherokee was parked in the driveway, so with Bible in hand, I knocked on the front door.

"Come on in, brother," he said, "I was about to throw a steak on the grill. Would you like one?"

"Sure, that would be great."

We spent an hour on the back porch, engaged in small talk during dinner. His backyard was filled with tall trees and rows of dense bushes and vines, which covered the pillars supporting his patio cover.

"Did you do the landscaping yourself?" I asked.

"No, I bought the house from an older couple. They must have worked day and night pulling weeds with all the flower gardens."

"I came over to talk about Romans. Did you get a chance to study Isaiah?"

"No, I haven't had time. What did you come up with?"

"In the book of Romans, Paul was writing to a

newly established church, selling the Jews on the New Covenant. Previously, the Jews were justified before God by performing the ceremonial laws and sin offerings as described in the books of Leviticus, Numbers and Deuteronomy.

"In Romans 3:28, Paul says, *For we hold that a person is justified by faith apart from works prescribed by the law.* That's because in the New Covenant, Jews and Gentiles now have the opportunity to be justified by faith in Jesus apart from the works of purification rituals. Paul never eliminated the Ten Commandments, because we are still required to be holy as God is holy."

"That's impossible! No one is that holy. Jesus fulfilled the law for us, and now we don't have to. All we need is faith in Jesus' obedience as a substitute for our own."

"Instead of getting into another argument, let's talk personally. You're my friend and brother in Christ. Tell me about your personal relationship with Jesus. It sounds like the day you get to Heaven, Saint Peter is going to ask you questions about Jesus. If you have the correct information, you'll be saved."

"That's correct, except I'm already saved. All have sinned and fallen short, and no one is holy enough to get into Heaven on their own accord. I'm saved by faith in Jesus, and that's exactly what I'm going to say when I reach the pearly white gates. What's your plan?"

"Same as yours. I'm here to see Jesus, let me in. But my confidence doesn't come from Bible quotes or magic information. It comes through personal relationship and steadfast obedience. I know when I'm in right relationship with the Lord because it's a function of my heart, not my intellect.

"Let me share some examples why I believe this. Are you open to hear me?"

"This ought to be good. Go ahead," Scott said.

"The first comes from the life of Paul. As you know, Paul was one of the Lord's greatest apostles. A quote from 2 Corinthians 11:23-28 describes his passion beautifully.

...with far greater labors, far more imprisonments, with countless floggings, and often near death. Five times I have received from the Jews the forty lashes minus one. Three times I was beaten with rods. Once I received a stoning. Three times I was shipwrecked; for a night and a day I was adrift at sea; on frequent journeys, in danger from rivers, danger from bandits, danger from my own people, danger from Gentiles, danger in the city, danger in the wilderness, danger at sea, danger from false brothers and sisters; in toil and hardship, through many a sleepless night, hungry and thirsty, often without food, cold and naked. And, besides other things, I am under daily pressure because of my anxiety for all the churches.

"Now let's look at how Paul describes his own walk. In 1 Corinthians 9:24-27, he compares himself to an Olympic athlete who must compete in a long-distance race and fight a treacherous boxing match.

Do you not know that in a race the runners all compete, but only one receives the prize? Run in such a way that you may win it. Athletes exercise self-control in all things; they do it to receive a perishable wreath, but we an imperishable one. So I do not run aimlessly, nor do I box as though beating the air; but I punish my body and enslave it, so that after proclaiming to others I myself should not be disqualified.

"If the only requirement to get into Heaven is a mere belief, why would this powerful man of God feel the need to punish and enslave his body to keep himself from being disqualified?"

"He probably felt bad for having Stephen stoned to death and through his guilt, became overzealous," Scott said.

"Then why does he tell Timothy the same thing? In 2 Timothy 1:5 it says, *I am reminded of your sincere faith, a faith that lived first in your grandmother Lois and your mother Eunice and now, I am sure, lives in you.*

"If Timothy already had *sincere faith* in Jesus, why would Paul tell him to pay close attention to his ministry if he wants to be saved? 1 Timothy 4:16: *Pay close attention to yourself and to your teaching; continue in these things, for in doing this you will save both yourself and your hearers.*

"Clearly Paul and Timothy believed the process of salvation is a lifelong journey that requires service and obedience to Christ."

"Then how do you explain Acts 16:25-31?" Scott asked.

About midnight Paul and Silas were praying and singing hymns to God, and the prisoners were listening to them. Suddenly there was an earthquake, so violent that the foundations of the prison were shaken; and immediately all the doors were opened and everyone's chains were unfastened. When the jailer woke up and saw the prison doors wide open, he drew his sword and was about to kill himself, since he supposed that the prisoners had escaped. But Paul shouted in a loud voice, 'Do not harm yourself, for we are all here.' The jailer called for lights, and rushing in, he fell down trembling before Paul and Silas. Then he brought them outside and said, *'Sirs, what must I do to be saved?' They answered, 'Believe on the Lord Jesus, and you will be saved, you and your household.'"*

"I would say the process of salvation is a past, present and future event, just like marriage. At one point in the jailer's walk, he married Jesus. Salvation like a marriage is also a present event, because in Philippians 2:12, Paul says, *...work out your own salvation with fear and trembling.* Notice the key words, *work out,* in the present tense. Just like, *work on* your marriage every day or else it may end in divorce.

"Salvation is also a future event. In Matthew 24:12-13, Jesus says, *...because of the increase of lawlessness, the love of many will grow cold. But the one who endures to the end will be saved.* If you don't endure to the end and continue to work out your salvation every day..."

"The thief on the cross," Scott said. "He lived a life of sin and at the last minute, entered into eternal rest."

"Jesus can grant salvation to whomever He wants, but what does that have to do with you? And how do you explain the most frightening verse in the Bible? In Matthew 7:21-23 Jesus describes Judgment Day.

Not everyone who says to me, 'Lord, Lord,' will enter the kingdom of heaven, but only the one who does the will of my Father in heaven. On that day many will say to me, 'Lord, Lord, did we not prophesy in your name, and cast out demons in your name, and do many deeds of power in your name?' Then I will declare to them, 'I never knew you; go away from me, you evildoers.'

"Jesus is not talking about the ungodly in this passage," I continued. "He's talking about people who were expecting to get into Heaven because they believed information about Him and had performed religious behaviors in His name. Not only did these people use His name to preach sermons, but they also worked many powerful deeds.

"What does Jesus tell these so-called Christians? I never knew you! You never developed personal relationship with me. You never listened to my voice. You never did the will of my Father in Heaven. Now get out of my sight, you deceived evildoers.

"My final point is from Matthew 7:13-14, where Jesus describes the Christian walk and the process that leads to salvation: *Enter through the narrow gate; for the gate is wide and the road is easy that leads to destruction, and there are many who take it. For the gate is narrow and the road is hard that leads to life, and there are few who find it.*

"My question to you, Scott — are you walking the hard and narrow road? Are you twisting Scripture out of context to create an easy road, or are you walking the hard and narrow road that leads to eternal life?"

"How dare you judge my walk. I graduated from Brighton Theological Seminary and you never graduated from high school. I'll give you a thought for the evening! 2 Peter 2:1-3:

But false prophets also arose among the people, just as there will be false teachers among you, who will secretly bring in destructive opinions. They will even deny the Master who bought them — bringing swift destruction on themselves. Even so, many will follow their licentious ways, and because of these teachers the way of truth will be maligned. And in their greed they will exploit you with deceptive words. Their condemnation, pronounced against them long ago, has not been idle, and their destruction is not asleep.

"That describes you perfectly! Now get out of my house!" he shouted.

Twenty-Seven

During the next several months, I continued working with the homeless population on the streets of Denver. My territory grew from Alameda and the Platte River to East Colfax, with the help of tiny yellow cards that read:

Need a new life?

Tired of life on the streets?

I will help you get a good job,

food and a roof over your head.

All in exchange for 2 weeks of time.

No money needed — Just call

After finding out the two-week exchange of time involved detox and self-work, very few homeless men were interested in my offer. Although, just receiving the invitation and knowing someone cared, brought many street brothers much joy. They would hold on to my number for months, and every so often, I would receive a call from someone who was serious.

Most of my ministry success came from personal relationship. Every day, I made the rounds and showed the street people God's love. With prayer and discernment, I searched for those whom the Lord wanted me to work with.

After introducing myself and listening to their stories, I learned where they spent their time and began visiting them on a regular basis. I developed personal relationships by stopping by two or three times a week, buying food and taking them shopping at thrift stores. I opened my heart in love, helped them talk through their childhood wounds and kept encouraging them along the road to recovery.

Before long, my reputation had grown, and some of the street brothers nicknamed me The Preacher because I kept handing out Gideon Bibles and asking them about God.

During this time, I had more of the Lord's anointing, peace and joy than at any other time in my life. I felt as though I was finally fulfilling God's calling. Someone could have offered me a million dollars for the joy I was experiencing with the Lord, and I would have told them, *No way!*

Then one day things took a turn for the worse. I was working the area of 6th and Galapago when I met a homeless man named Van, who wanted money for a pager. He was clean-cut with short hair, had a great personality and traveled around on a bicycle.

"Why do you need a pager?" I asked.

"I want to start a handyman repair business and get myself off the streets. In Oregon, I went door-to-door with flyers and had all kinds of work. But now, there's no way for anyone to call me."

"What if I made some flyers with my cell number? I'll answer the phone and help sell the job. After you complete all the work, you'll have your own money for a pager."

"Sounds like a winner," Van said. "When can I get the flyers?"

"I'll bring some tomorrow. Let's meet at 10 a.m. in that park over there."

"My old flyers read, *Rip Van Winkle Construction, Repairs, Remodeling and Siding.* I hang a lot of vinyl siding. I also had pictures of a hammer and a miniature saw. Can you do that?"

"I'm no graphic artist, but I'll see what the clip-art has to offer."

When I arrived to meet Van the following day, he was waiting underneath a picnic shelter with another guy, who smelled like he had been drinking all night. He had long black hair and tattoos all over both arms and was cussing up a storm.

"I got some more help," Van said. "His name's Striker. He's going to be working with us."

"You look like you're freezing, Striker. Don't you have a coat?"

"Nah, man. All my gear got ripped off last week."

"Van, we need to talk... In private."

After walking a short distance away, I handed Van the flyers and said, "Drinking is going to be a major problem."

"I already told him none of that on the job site.

Besides, we need someone to do the work. I'm fifty-five years old. You know, a little drink here and there, ain't going to hurt anyone."

"Have it your way. It's your handyman service, responsibility and liability. I'll help you sell the job and get some tools, but the rest is up to you."

"Don't worry," Van said as I turned to leave.

Several hours later, I received a call from Van saying, "We're over at Albertson's parking lot handing out flyers. We're almost out, can you bring more?"

"Sure, give me a couple hours."

When I arrived, Van was talking to a lady named Rebecca. She wanted a six-foot privacy fence built in her backyard. It sounded like the perfect job. There were no steep roofs to fall from and nothing that required a lot of skill or precision. It was just hard physical labor where nothing could go wrong.

After I introduced myself, Rebecca said, "Will you please follow me to the property and give an estimate right away? I need to be out of my old house in two weeks and need the work completed on the new place before I move in."

"I didn't bring a tape measure, but I'd be happy to take a look," I said.

Upon arriving, she showed me the dilapidated chain link fence that enclosed the backyard. The fence posts were on eight-foot centers. I counted twenty-two of them and quickly figured 180 feet of fencing would be needed. Without checking lumber prices, I calculated $5 per post, $3 per bag of cement and $28 for premanufactured picket sections.

Rebecca was open to used materials, so I quoted her $1,600. We negotiated back and forth and finally settled on $1,500. I was overjoyed and couldn't wait to tell Van.

"I sold your first job," I said, after locating him in the Albertson's parking lot. "$800 for materials and $700 for labor. Once the job's complete, you'll have enough for a pager and an apartment. You and Striker can be roommates. Isn't that great? Within a week, you'll be off the streets!"

"Sounds like a winner," he said. "We'll need $20 a day advance for food and stuff. When can we start?"

"Tomorrow. I have a 9 a.m. appointment with Rebecca to sign the contract. After she pays half down, I'll drop you and Striker off at the job to start tearing down the old fence."

"What about tools?" Van asked.

"Don't worry. A couple of hammers, string line, shovels, a wheelbarrow, I'll bring everything you'll need."

"Didn't that lady say her house was in Aurora? How are we going to get back and forth from work?" Van asked.

"I thought you could sleep on the floor, since her house is vacant. I even have a couple of thrift store sleeping bags you can borrow."

"Sounds like a winner."

The next day, after the homeowner signed the contract, I worked with Van and Striker all morning to get them started. I laid out the new fence with a string line and marked the post holes with stakes.

"All you have to do is finish tearing down the old fence and dig the new post holes. Make sure they're all two feet deep. If you finish, go ahead and start setting them in concrete. I'll be back tomorrow."

"Before you go, we need our $20 a day advance to buy lunch. I'm already out of cigarettes."

"All I have is $30, you'll have to split it."

"Sounds like a winner," Van said, taking the money from my hand.

When I arrived early the next morning, I knew something was wrong. The front door had been left open and I noticed muddy footprints all over the hardwood floors. They were coming from the bathroom, where a puddle of water was overflowing into the hallway.

Rushing to see what was wrong, I found the toilet plugged with human waste and newspapers. It looked like it had been running all night, because the hardwood floors were swollen and starting to buckle.

When I turned the water off, I could hear the sound of something dripping from the basement. Running downstairs, I slipped and fell on the wet tile. I couldn't figure out why pieces of plaster were scattered all over, until I looked up. Water from the upstairs toilet had broken through the drywall ceiling.

Still in shock, I went outside to find Van and Striker.

They were attempting to set an eight-foot post in a

six-inch hole. They had it propped up with little sticks when I walked over and ripped it out of the ground. Hurling it across the yard I screamed, "These holes need to be two feet deep! You were supposed to tear down the old fence and finish the dirt work. Not waste a bag of concrete!"

"The dirt's too hard. You try digging it," Van said.

"That's exactly why drunks are not allowed on the job site!"

"The hell with you! I'm out of here," Van said, as he stormed off.

Turning to Striker, I said, "Are you quitting too?"

"Nah, man. I need the money."

"Then find some rags and clean the crap out of the toilet before the homeowner discovers what happened."

After calming down, I got down on my hands and knees and helped Striker clean up the mess. We worked all day repairing drywall and repainting the ceiling. Eventually, the hardwood floor settled back down, and with the help of a few nails, it looked as good as new.

After work that evening, Striker didn't have anywhere to stay, so I gave him a ride to the overnight shelter and said, "Wait in line. At 8 p.m. they'll feed you dinner and give you a mat on the floor."

"Are we working tomorrow?"

"I have a 10 a.m. appointment and it's going to take a couple of hours. If you want, I'll pick you up at noon."

"I'll be here," Striker said. "Can I get my advance?"

"I think you already spent your advance on the hardwood floors."

Twenty-Eight

~⊙†☾~

The next day, I arrived at my appointment early. I desperately needed to talk with someone, and as soon as I got inside Dr. Patterson's office, I described how Van and Striker destroyed the inside of Rebecca's house. "They even burned my sleeping bags," I said.

"How did that happen?" she asked.

"After work, they got drunk in a field around a campfire. Apparently they ran out of firewood, so Van threw the sleeping bags in for fuel. After the fire department left, they passed out drunk on the kitchen floor."

"Can you see past Van's behavior and into his hurt?" she asked.

"Give me a break. It happened yesterday and I'm still hurt. I wanted to give the sleeping bags to guys who are freezing to death outside."

"It will help you move past your own hurt when you acknowledge the hurt in others."

"I know they're both really good guys and that alcohol is to blame. Satan loves playing with drunk men. But sometimes it's hard separating the sinner from their sickening behavior."

"I know it's hard. What are you going to do?"

"I have to finish the job. I'm responsible, because I took the homeowner's money. I'll get some more guys and build her a quality fence on schedule. It just makes me mad! Back when I built townhomes, I would have never allowed a drunk on the job site. Now, I'm losing money with a homeless labor force. Go figure."

"What did the Lord say about the fence project?"

"That's the problem. I didn't specifically ask, the job just fell together. I know He has called me into homeless work. I can feel His peaceful presence and can see Him working in the lives of the men. But whenever I inquire about the direction of my life, He's been silent."

"Let me give an example from my past," Dr. Patterson said. "After graduation, I was faced with a difficult decision. I wanted to open a private practice and help others grow spiritually; but a prestigious hospital on the East Coast kept pursuing me with a high-paying job offer.

"I sought the Lord's direction day and night, but didn't hear anything. He was silent. I felt the Lord pulling back because He wanted me to make my own decision. Would I serve Him through hardships and financial difficulties or take a high-paying secular job?

"I feel the same things happening in your life. After surrendering your life and learning about ministry, you have a choice to make. You're not a puppet. God is not going to make all your decisions for you."

"I've already made that decision. I'm going after the Lord with everything I've got. I don't care if it's healing seminars, book promotion or homeless ministry. I just want the Lord to use my life powerfully.

"When I stand in front of the throne on Judgment Day, I don't want to have any regrets. From here on out, I'm promoting the Kingdom day and night."

"Maybe the Lord has answered your heart's cry and is stretching your abilities?" Dr. Patterson suggested.

"What do you mean?"

"Do you remember last year when you were struggling with the speed limit? How you didn't have the internal strength to be obedient without the Lord's help?"

"How could I forget?"

"The same thing applies to ministry. Without the Lord's help you don't have the power to love and serve the homeless. John 15:4-6 describes it beautifully.

Abide in me as I abide in you. Just as the branch cannot bear fruit by itself unless it abides in the vine, neither can you unless you abide in me. I am the vine, you are the branches. Those who abide in me and I in them bear much fruit, because apart from me you can do nothing. Whoever does not abide in me is thrown away like a branch and withers; such branches are gathered, thrown into the fire, and burned.

"The problem is, no one has the power to bear fruit on their own. That's why ministry and personal relationship flow together in a continuous cycle. Jesus calls everyone into ministry knowing they don't have the power. When we rely on the Lord's strength, He will stretch our abilities and give us the power to produce more and more fruit."

"*Stretched* is the word! I felt like killing those guys. I hate to say this, but five years ago I would have taken a two-by-four after them."

"I just love watching the Lord work in your life. It's people like you that make me glad I never took the hospital job on the East Coast. I know it's hard being stretched, but the Lord is faithful to His promise: *Every branch that bears fruit He prunes to make it bear more fruit.*"

"Thanks again, Dr. Patterson. I feel much better."

"I'll keep the fence job in my prayers," she said. "Let me give you a verse from Matthew 10:42 before you go: *...whoever gives even a cup of cold water to one of these little ones in the name of a disciple — truly I tell you, none of these will lose their reward.*"

Twenty-Nine

*A*fter leaving Dr. Patterson's office, I drove to the overnight shelter looking for Striker. I waited in front of the building until well past noon, but he was nowhere to be found. I didn't want to build the fence by myself, so I asked two men sitting next to a pile of pallets in the back alley if they wanted to work.

"Sure, we'll do anything," one of them said.

"Have you guys been drinking?"

"No, I just got out of detox this morning, and that's where I met Bill," one of them said.

"What's your name?"

"I'm Jeff. We were just talking about work."

"Why are you guys just sitting around?"

"The detox van dropped us off this morning," Bill said.

"Sobriety Center has a thirty-day program, but there's a waiting list," Jeff said.

"Let's go, my truck's out front. We'll be building a fence all day. I'll bring you back here tonight."

Bill and Jeff worked hard all morning. We rented a gas-powered auger, and by early afternoon, had all the posts set in concrete.

Sitting on the back porch during lunch, it felt like the hard physical labor had formed a bond between us. It was Bill's job to align the posts with a string and make sure they were level. Jeff was responsible for mixing the concrete and keeping it the proper consistency. They both took great pride in their workmanship, knowing the homeowner would be pleased with their efforts.

The next day as we were installing rails, I was able to connect with Bill and Jeff on a deeper level. We spoke about a personal relationship with Jesus, and their future plans.

They were both struggling with temptations of alcohol, so I said, "It will be necessary to take every thought captive."

"Say what?"

"If you want to stop drinking, you'll need to stand against evil with the Lord's strength. After surrendering your life and heart to Jesus, overcoming the battleground of the mind should be your next priority.

"Let's use the example of nailing pickets. Your body doesn't automatically start nailing pickets without your permission. A command from your thoughts occurs before your arm starts swinging the hammer. The thought process happens so quietly, it might seem automatic, but your mind is in control at all times.

"The same thing happened in the Garden of Eden. The serpent was able to deceive Eve by inserting tempting thoughts into her mind. No one forced Eve to eat the apple, she made a decision based on the information inside her head. All Eve had to do was rebuke Satan and cast the sinful thought aside.

"It also applies to drinking. When thoughts about using enter your mind, take them captive. Command them to flee in the name, power and authority of Jesus. Instead of thinking about how good alcohol makes you feel, try focusing on all the destruction it has caused.

"Fill your mind with positive thoughts just like Philippians 4:8: *...whatever is true, whatever is honorable, whatever is just, whatever is pure, whatever is pleasing, whatever is commendable, if there is any excellence and if there is anything worthy of praise, think about these things."*

"I never understood that before," Bill said. "They call it 'stinking thinking' in AA, but it never made sense."

"Why don't you guys practice your affirmations every time you nail a picket on the fence? Either say something good about yourself or give a reason why you hate alcohol. I'll be working on the back gate, if you need anything."

From across the yard I could hear Bill and Jeff barking out their affirmations like military drill sergeants. They were working harder and faster than ever.

"I hate alcohol because it makes you stupid!"

"I hate alcohol because I fall down and get hurt."

As I watched them nailing pickets on the fence, I felt an overwhelming desire to start a construction company called Homeless Homebuilders. Not only would the work be performed by recovering alcoholics and street people, but it would also be a discipleship program. A place where guys could heal their emotional issues, work hard, save money and rebuild their lives.

Later that afternoon, Bill and Jeff were nailing on the last few pickets when I called them over and said, "Would you guys be interested in fixing up an old house? I know where one's for sale. You could live and work there the same time."

"That would be great!" Jeff said.

"Yeah, I was wondering if you had anything else lined up," Bill said.

"I'll keep working with you, if you keep working with me."

As we rolled up the tools that evening, I got a call from Cindy on the cell phone. She said, "I have the most incredible invitation for you."

"What?"

"Some friends of mine are visiting from Nashville and they're leading worship at the Easter sunrise service. They have a phenomenal band and backstage passes, and afterwards, we're all going to brunch at Brandon's."

"I would love to, but I already have plans."

"Can you rework them? It's going to be great."

"I wish I could, but I invited the Lord to join me on the boat. He has already confirmed the appointment in my prayer time. I know something big is going to happen."

Well, in that case," Cindy said. "What happens if it's rainy, will you still go?"

"If something changes, I'll call."

"Be careful, I love you."

"Love ya too. Bye."

Thirty

Early Easter morning, long before sunrise, I backed my truck to the trailer and connected the hitch. I had prepared all my favorite foods the night before. I placed the cooler in the back of the boat and headed for the reservoir.

Upon my arrival, I carefully backed down the ramp and launched the boat into the calm, dimly lit waters. By the soft glow of the moon, I had enough light to secure a line to the dock. Ever so gracefully, the boat rocked back and forth as I pulled the trailer out of the water and parked it in a nearby lot.

I was in luck. The boat started without any mechanical difficulties, and after allowing it to warm up, I proceeded towards the center of the lake.

Slowly, I navigated underneath the star-filled sky, across waters smooth as glass. A gentle breeze carried a springtime scent through the air, while the slap of water against the hull created a tranquil, serene rhythm.

Quietly I waited.

As the morning light softly dissolved the darkness, I knew sunrise was close at hand. The thin clouds that floated along the eastern horizon were beginning to change colors. The gray tones slowly gave way to pastel shades of pink and orange.

Suddenly, I felt the presence of the Lord. "I'm here," He said softly.

"Oh Lord, I love you. I give you my life!"

"Do you really love me?" He asked.

His words stabbed deep in my heart. I felt like Peter when Jesus asked him the same thing three times. I wanted to go home and cry. It didn't seem fair. It was Easter morning, and everybody else was experiencing fuzzy bunnies in church, while I received the spirit of conviction in the middle of a lake.

After sitting in silence and processing my hurt feelings, I realized the Lord was right. I hadn't given Him everything. Many years ago when I built townhomes, I worked fourteen hours a day. With unstoppable passion, I drove my laborers and injured my body in the process. When I ran out of money and needed a construction loan, I hit the banks, knocked down doors and defeated any obstacle to prevent a financial loss. I had given the pursuit of money all of my passion, but when it came time to feed His sheep and tend the flock, I found myself holding back and making excuses.

Getting down on my knees, I started to pray, "I'm sorry, Lord. Please forgive me. I feel like the worthless servant who has done no more than what was asked. Please remove all ungodly hindrances and worldly vanities from my life. Increase my ability to love and serve your people. Break me and fill me with your compassionate presence. Wrap your loving arms around me, Abba Father."

As I continued praying, the Lord filled my heart with His euphoric peace. Looking up, I saw the radiant glow of the sun breaking over the horizon. Its brilliant rays illuminated the heavens as He asked a familiar question from years past. "Will you endure until the end?"

Epilogue

PASSAGE 1

Hebrews 11:6 says, *...without faith it is impossible to please God...* Abraham, the father of faith, was called by God at age seventy-five to leave his home. He lived in a tent, as an alien in a land experiencing a severe famine. I'm sure Abraham wondered why God wanted him to *wander from his father's house,* but he held fast and continued to walk in faith.

Years later God told Abraham to circumcise his entire household. I'm sure every male servant questioned Abraham's calling from God. But he held fast and walked in faith.

After Abraham waited twenty-five years for Isaac to be born, God said, take your son, whom you love, and offer him as a burnt offering. I'm sure Abraham didn't feel like setting his child on fire. I'm sure he wanted to question or even disobey God's command, but he didn't. Abraham continued to walk in faith. Bone crushing, flesh ripping faith, and in Genesis 15:6, *...the Lord reckoned it to him as righteousness.*

PASSAGE 2

There are many different levels of freedom from sin. The first is when you're sorry that God's laws are in direct conflict with your behaviors. The next is where you enjoy sinful behavior and keep running back to God and asking forgiveness. The next is when you refuse to commit a sin, but because of alluring attractions, open doors and lies planted by the enemy, you find yourself constantly tempted.

True freedom comes from loving God's laws more than life itself. When you reach this level, your eyes are open to the destruction sin causes and you want nothing to do with evil. Instead of turning to your sinful behavior to satisfy your needs, turn to God with the same hunger.

PASSAGE 3

Matthew 5:48 says: *Be perfect, therefore, as your heavenly Father is perfect.* Before you'll be able to follow this command, it will be necessary to examine your conscience on a daily basis. If you fail to acknowledge your sinfulness before God, it's very easy to grow accustomed to evil and fall into a pattern of complacent stagnation.

By examining your actions and attitudes every day, you'll be able to identify recurring patterns of sinfulness. Day after day you may find yourself struggling with the same temptations. But over time, if you truly seek freedom and God's assistance, you'll have permanent victory in Christ.

PASSAGE 4

I had to be seriously broken before surrendering my life over to the Lord. The process came in many steps. First, I trusted Him with tithing, then I surrendered my self-employed business life. Next, I gave Him my sex life and finally, my heart.

Looking back, I'm very glad I lost a quarter million dollars trading commodities, because now, I'm blessed with true riches. Being in a right relationship with God is worth more than anything this world has to offer.

Have you surrendered every aspect of your life over to the Lord Jesus Christ? Are you holding anything back? Take a minute right now and dig down deep inside your heart. What would happen if He removed all your finances, relationships and worldly agendas? Would you be content with His love?

He has an incredible plan for your life, and you will not be able to fulfill it unless you come to Him in complete surrender. Leave your self-directed life behind. Come into His incredible love and experience your calling.

PASSAGE 5

Ephesians 6:10-17 commands every Christian to put on the armor of God. Put it on, keep it on and never take it off. Put on the biblical belt of truth. Satan is *a liar and the father of lies* and by planting one complacent lie in your mind, evil can throw your Christian walk way off course. Put on the breastplate of righteous and sinless living. Put on the shield of faith like Abraham wore.

Finally, carry around a powerful weapon, the sword, which is the Word of God. By studying the Bible in the same context that the author intended for its original audience, you'll be better protected from Satan's lies. The truth will set you free, and the best way to acquire truth is the daily reading of Scripture.

PASSAGE 6

Whenever you find yourself tempted to sin, it's important to call on the name of Jesus. When you do, Jesus will give you the power to overcome the enemy and stand victorious. Simply give the command out loud, *"I take authority over my heart, mind, body, soul, spirit, environment and command all evil to flee in the name of Jesus."* After you repeat this command several times, the temptation will quickly subside.

Try to exhibit the fruits of the Spirit at all times — love, joy, peace, patience, kindness, generosity, faithfulness, gentleness and self-control. Whenever you're not exhibiting the fruits, stop yourself and take every thought into captive obedience through Jesus Christ.

PASSAGE 7

Deuteronomy 18:9-14 specifically forbids God's people from practicing witchcraft, divination, fortune-telling, spirit guide channeling, seeking oracles from the dead, or casting spells. Many times in an attempt to be more spiritual, Christians read New Age books and horoscopes, study astrology, have their palms read, study world religions, play with a ouiji board or tarot cards. When doing so, you are opening yourself up to the demonic.

Satan disguises himself as an angel of light in hopes of alluring people into something beneficial. When you seek information about your life through a spirit guide, instead of receiving a benefit, you are communicating with a demon. It's extremely important to search the past, renounce anything of the occult and destroy all charms, games, artifacts and books within your possession.

PASSAGE 8

Almost all secular radio and television programming contains antibiblical and ungodly messages. Musical lyrics glamorize fairy-tale relationships, and seductive commercials show the audience how to obtain ultimate happiness in life. Even after minimal exposure to this type of programming, I find subliminal messages getting trapped into my subconscious.

By turning the television completely off, I was able to transform what would have been two hours of brainwashing nonsense into deep passionate intimacy with the Lord Jesus Christ. I started with a forty-day commitment during lent. Instead of watching all the things God hates on television, I spent that time pouring my heart out in prayer. Lying underneath the star-filled night sky wrapped in blankets, I discovered how to commune with the Lover of my soul.

PASSAGE 9

In 1 Kings 19:9-13, Elijah did not find God in the strong wind, the earthquake or the fire, but in the sound of sheer silence. The best way to hear from God is to schedule time in complete silence, practicing contemplative prayer. Quiet all your thoughts and focus your complete attention on the divine presence of Jesus. When you do this, God will fill you with His peace, guidance and direction.

Using a prayer log is also an effective way to keep your prayer life strong. Try writing down a specific prayer regarding another person's situation and pray using Scripture. Many times God answers prayers weeks later, and if you have a written log, you'll be able to see God move more clearly through the power of prayer.

PASSAGE 10

Fasting is a direct pipeline into the presence of God. Fasting will give you power over fleshly, selfish desires and allow you to hear from God on difficult decisions. It also helps break recurring sins and fight demonic strongholds. Fasting is not about dieting, it's about denying yourself and seeking God with everything you've got.

There are many books available on the power of fasting, and medically speaking, it's healthy for the human body. Begin the process by skipping a meal and spending the time in prayer. You'll notice a considerable difference in your closeness to God. Come, experience a real banquet. Strengthen your spirit with heavenly cuisine and indulge yourself with His divine presence.

PASSAGE 11

The most powerful work I have accomplished as a Christian is self-work. I had to go back into my past and make amends, ask forgiveness, heal open wounds and eliminate unhealthy childhood conditioning. I have spent many years working through the healing process and releasing all my repressed emotions. By embracing my negative emotions and lifting them to the Lord, I have found His love slowly washes away the pain.

Who do you need to forgive? Do you have any past memories that bring up negative feelings? Begin the journey towards emotional freedom by making a list of the worst experiences you have ever encountered. Take one situation at a time, vent the negative emotions and allow God's love into your hurt. By doing so, you'll break the bonds of unhealthy childhood conditioning and experience a newfound freedom in Christ's love.

PASSAGE 12

Christians are called to produce fruit through good works of love and charity, because Luke 3:9 says: *...every tree therefore that does not bear good fruit is cut down and thrown into the fire.* Consider setting a goal to dedicate one day a week for ministry above and beyond the normal work you perform unto the Lord.

There's no better way to know the heart of Christ than serving another. When you give of yourself you make room for more of the Lord's love and power to flow through your life. Why toil after earthly pleasure when you can experience the rich blessings of His heav-

enly treasure? Come, experience the depth and richness
of Christ through service to others.

PASSAGE 13

I started trusting the Lord with my finances the day I
put $287 in the church collection basket. After seeing the
power of God through a harvest yellow clothes dryer, I
started setting higher and higher tithing goals. Year after
year, God blessed my efforts tremendously. Some years
He doubled my income, other times He stripped everything away.

Not only is it important to give to God what belongs
to God, but to trust Him with every aspect of your
financial well being. Why withhold 10 percent? Luke
6:38 says, *give, and it will be given to you. A good measure,
pressed down, shaken together, running over, will be put into your
lap; for the measure you give will be the measure you get back.*

PASSAGE 14

John 13:34-35 says: *I give you a new commandment, that you
love one another. Just as I have loved you, you also should love one
another. By this everyone will know that you are my disciples, if you
have love for one another.* Love is what motivates people to
change. Love softens the hardest of hearts. It uplifts,
comforts, supports and validates. Love encourages, for-
gives, accepts and understands.

Have you removed the protective walls from your
heart that prevent the flow of love? Have you allowed
your loved ones inside your heart? God is love, and
when you open your heart to others in love, you'll expe-

rience more of His divine presence. The more love you give, the more love you will receive. God has an endless supply. You can be the most loving person in the world, all you need to do is open up your heart.

PASSAGE 15

Dying to self — getting the desires of your flesh under control and leaving the ways of the world behind — is not easily done. It's a long hard journey that all Christians are required to make on a daily basis. One way to begin the process is to pray to be broken. *Lord, if there's any material possessions that I put before you, please remove them from me. Lord, if I'm traveling on any road that I shouldn't be on, please slam the door in my face. Lord, if it's not your will for me to be in relationship with this person, please remove him or her from my life.*

What are you waiting for? Time is short. Join the race and find out how much of God you can experience in a lifetime. Why chase after worldly vanities and ungodly relationships? They will never fill the empty void deep in your soul. There's only one way, and that's through the heart of Christ — Himself.

PASSAGE 16

Christian fellowship is significant because God's love is experienced through fellow brothers and sisters. Making a commitment to a church, attending Bible studies, fellowship meetings, volunteering at Christian events, developing a close inner circle of friends, praying together, encouraging one another and ministering together are all powerful ways to receive the necessary support required to complete the journey.

Regular church attendance is a requirement for all Christians, because James 4:17 says: *Anyone, then, who knows the right thing to do and fails to do it, commits sin.*

PASSAGE 17

When you open up your heart to Jesus in total surrender His divine presence will enter into the core of your being. Your head knowledge will turn into a passionate, heartfelt relationship. There's only room for one Captain of the heart, and He doesn't force Himself on anyone.

Can you remember a time when the presence of Christ entered into your heart? Have you become a new creation in Christ? Take the time today to look deep inside your heart. If there are any hindrances, ask Jesus to destroy them. Jesus may have to do a lot of work on your heart before you're ready. Don't give up, seek after Him day and night. Surrender everything over to Him with complete sincerity. He will honor your request. He's calling you right now. Come experience His love. Come experience the heart of Christ — Himself.

AUTHOR BIOGRAPHY

The author's greatest qualification to write this book is an obedient Christian walk. He never graduated from a prestigious university. In fact, he's a high school dropout. When he was twenty he served time in jail for acquiring a fake driver's license. He started working construction for minimum wage and at age twenty-eight, had lost more than a quarter million dollars of his hard-earned money trading high-risk commodities.

It was then the Lord called him to leave the ways of the world behind and write his first book. Now he's a Christian counselor, who seeks to know the heart of God and serves the homeless population of Denver, Colorado.

He has requested his name be withheld to accredit all the glory to his heavenly Father.